THE BIG
GET READY
BOOK

Author
Barbara Gregorich

Editor
Joan Hoffman

Designer/Artist
Richard Pape

The Big **Get Ready** Book is a compilation of favorite titles from the Get Ready series. The ten titles are listed on the table of contents.

CONTENTS

PARENT GUIDE

The skills covered in the Big Get Ready Book are those most commonly taught at the preschool level and in beginning first grade. Here are some suggestions for working with your child at home:

- Don't do too many pages at one sitting. Praise each completed page. Page by page, day to day, is best.

- If your child is puzzled by one activity, move on to another. The activities are ordered, but there's nothing magical about that order.

- Do the activities at a particular time of day, perhaps before snack time. Do them when the child is not tired. Discuss the learning experience. "Lets work in our school books today! Do you remember what you did yesterday?"

- Enjoy it! Laugh a lot! Discuss the activity. Most activities can be done independently by the child since directions are clear and consistent. Never use an activity as punishment. Don't expect too much. The activities are meant as practice.

- There will be days when your child may not feel like working. This is typical, so accept it. And remember: the communication patterns you establish today will pay off as your child grows older.

Draw a  around the and around the .

Draw a ⁓ from the to the .

3

Draw a  around the .

 the .

Draw a ☐ around the 🐟🐟🐟 .

Draw a 〰 from the 🎣 to the ⌇ .

Draw a around the .

Draw a around the .

Draw a ▭ around the .

the

Draw an  around the ⛏ and the 🚣 .

Draw a ⌒ from the 📦 to the 🦅 .

Draw a _____ from the to the .

 the .

Draw a  around the ⬭.

Draw a ☐ around the 🧍 and the ⬭.

Draw an ⬭ around the 🦨.

🖍 the 🌳.

11

Draw a 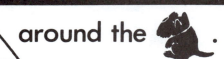 around the .

Draw a ⌒ from the to the .

Draw an ⬭ around the 🛠.

🖍 the 👒.

Draw a ▢ around the .

Draw a △ around the 🍦 and the 🐈.

Draw a  from the to the 🐕.

🖍 the ⚾🏏.

Draw a ⟋ from the  to the .

the and the .

Draw a ☐ around the 🍇 .

✏️ the 🍎 .

Draw a ◯ around the .

Draw a △ around the 🐱.

Draw an ⬭ around the 🦀.

Draw a ⟍ from the 🐦 to the .

Draw a ▭ around the 🔍.

Draw a △ around the 🐕.

Draw a △ around the ▱▱.

Draw a ⟍ from the 🌰 to the 🐻 .

Draw a ☐ around the .

© School Zone Publishing Company

Draw a ☐ around the 🚲 .

Draw a △ around the 🚲 .

Draw an ⬭ around the 🎺 and the 🥁.

Draw a ⌒ from the 🎺 to the 👟👟.

Draw a ☐ around the ⬭.

Draw a ╱ from the ◯ to the 🐭.

Draw a ◯ around the .

🖍 the 🦅.

Draw a  around the ⬜.

Draw a ⸺ from the 🐱 to the 🎨.

Draw a ☐ around the 🪰.

🖍 the 🌼.

Draw a _____ from the 🅐 to the ⚾ .

🖍 the 🦘 and the 🦘 .

Draw an ◯ around the  and the .

Draw a ▢ around the .

Draw a _____ from the 🐱 to the 🐶 .

🖍 the 🧣 .

Circle the picture that is the **same** as the first one.

Circle the picture that is the **same** as the first one.

Circle the picture that is the **same** as the first one.

Circle the **2** that are the **same**.

Circle the **2** that are the **same** in each group.

36

Circle the **2** that are the **same**.

Circle the **2** that are the **same** in each group.

Circle the **2** that are the **same**.

Circle the **2** that are the **same** in each group.

Circle the **2** that are the **same**.

Circle the **2** that are the **same** in each group.

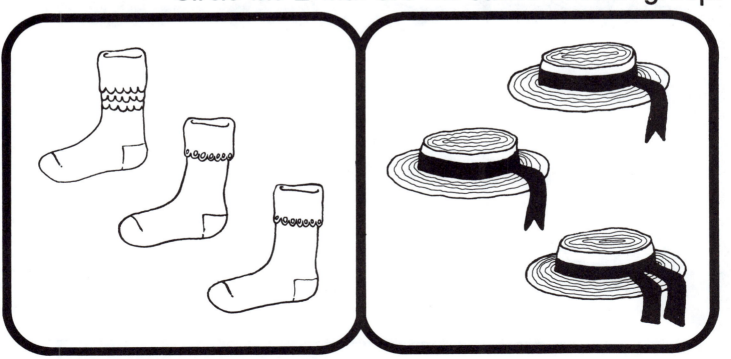

Circle the picture that is the **same size** as the first one.

Circle the picture that is the **same size** as the first one.

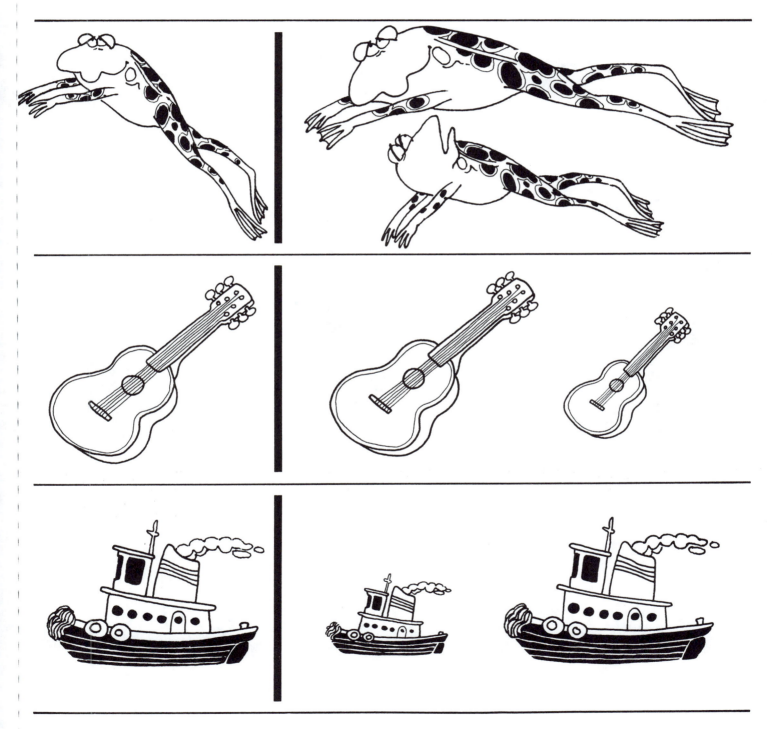

Circle the picture that is the **same** as the first one.

Circle the picture that is the **same** as the first one.

Circle the picture that is the **same** as the first one.

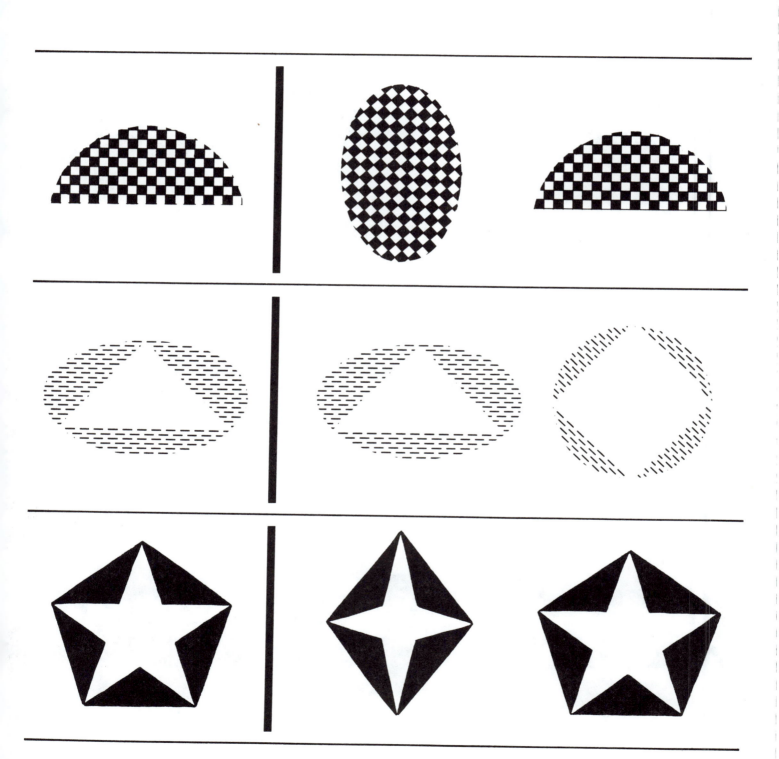

Circle the letters that are the **same** as the first two.

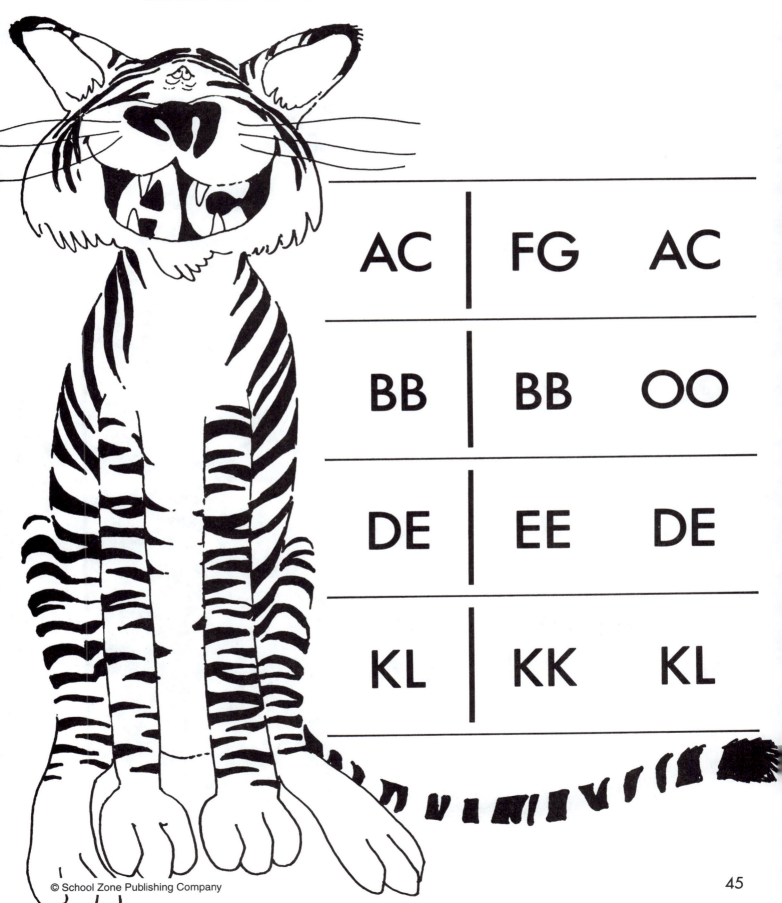

AC	FG	AC
BB	BB	OO
DE	EE	DE
KL	KK	KL

Circle the letters that are the **same** as the first two.

OP	OP	ER
RA	RS	RA
TU	UT	TU
WI	WI	WE

Circle the letters that are the same as the first two.

QT	OE	QT
VV	VV	WV
LS	LS	SL
XK	RK	XK

Circle the word that is the **same as the first word.**

IN	GO	IN
RUN	LET	RUN
SEE	SEE	CAT
DO	BE	DO

Circle the picture that is **different**.

Circle the picture that is **different**.

Circle the picture that is **different**.

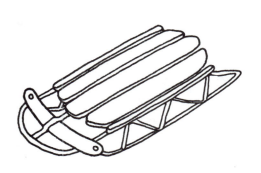

Circle the picture that is **different**.

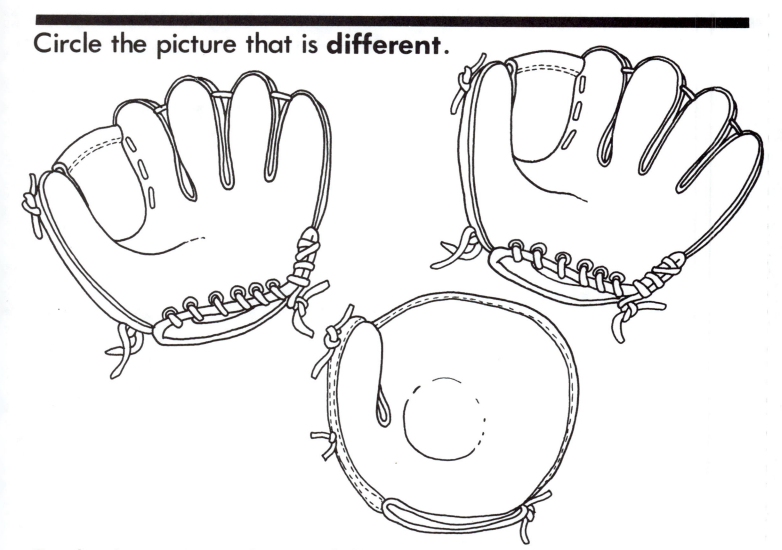

Circle the picture that is **different** in each group.

52

Circle the picture that is **different**.

Circle the picture that is **different** in each group.

Circle the picture that is **different**.

Circle the picture that is **different** in each group.

Circle the picture that is **different**.

Circle the picture that is **different** in each group.

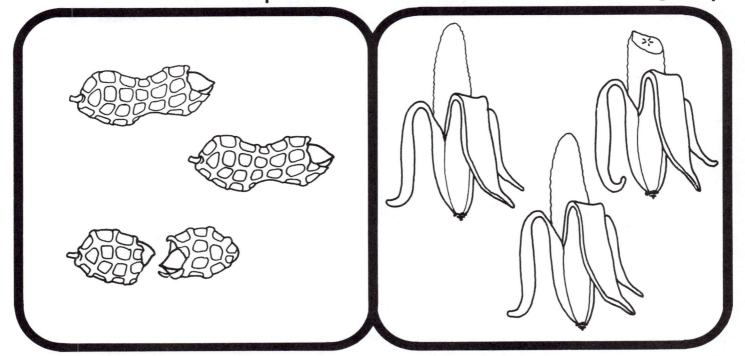

Circle the picture that is a **different size**.

Circle the picture that is a **different size.**

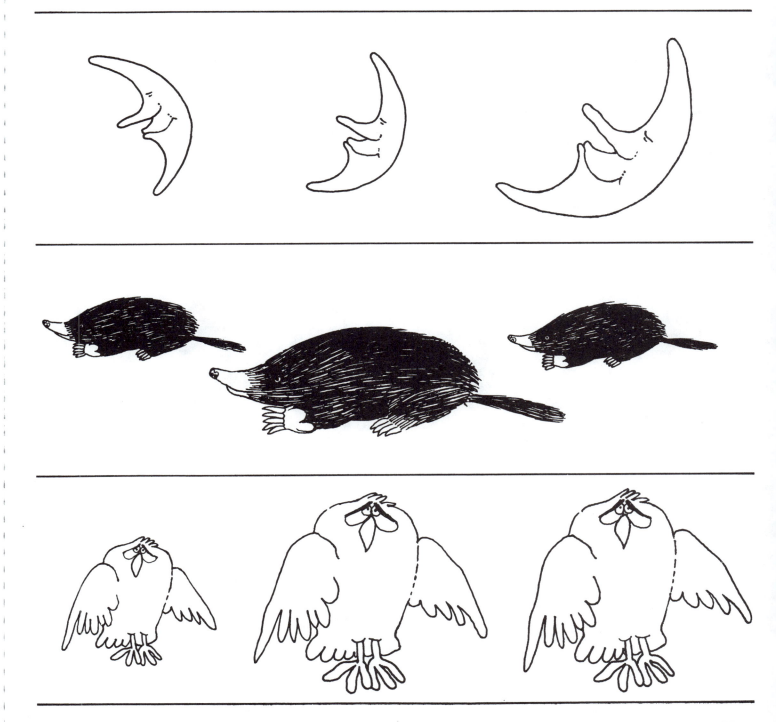

Circle the picture that is **different**.

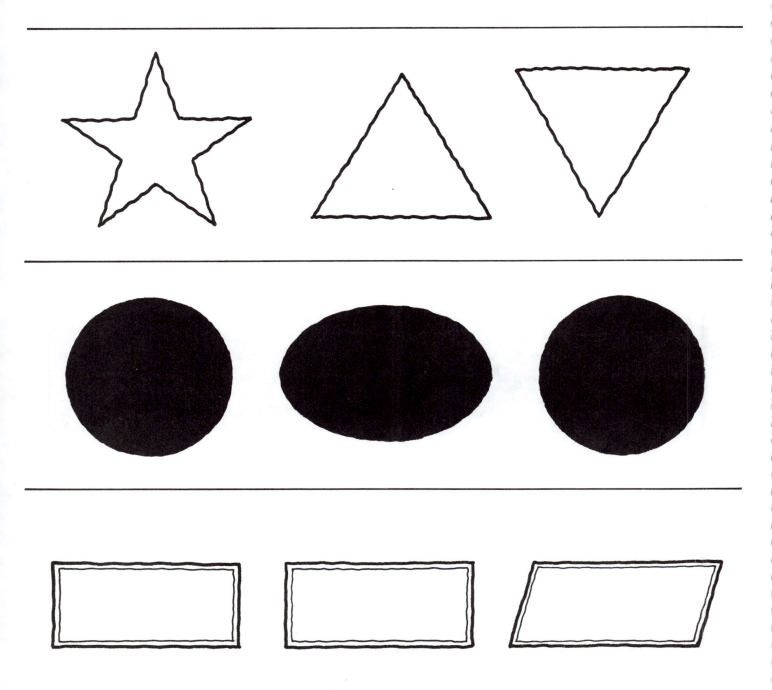

Circle the picture that is **different**.

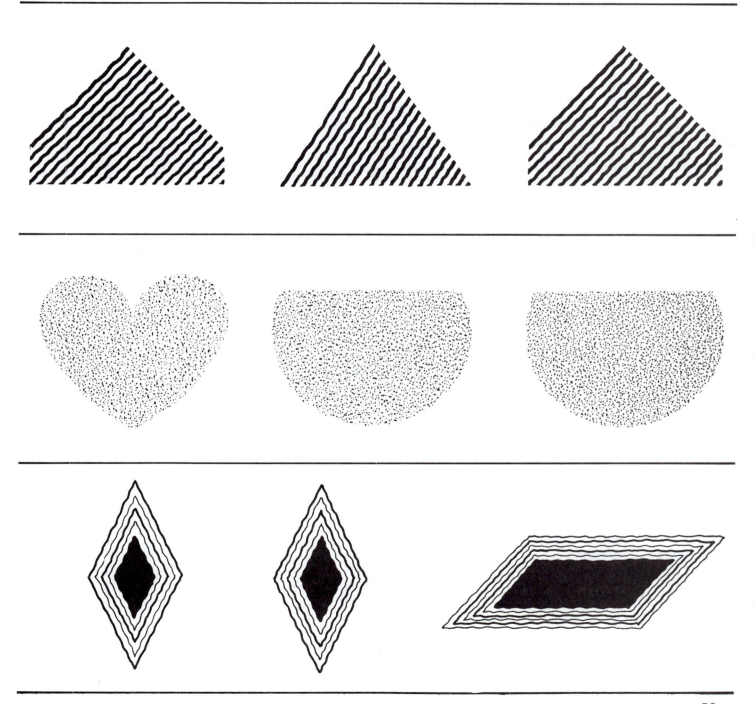

Circle the picture that is **different**.

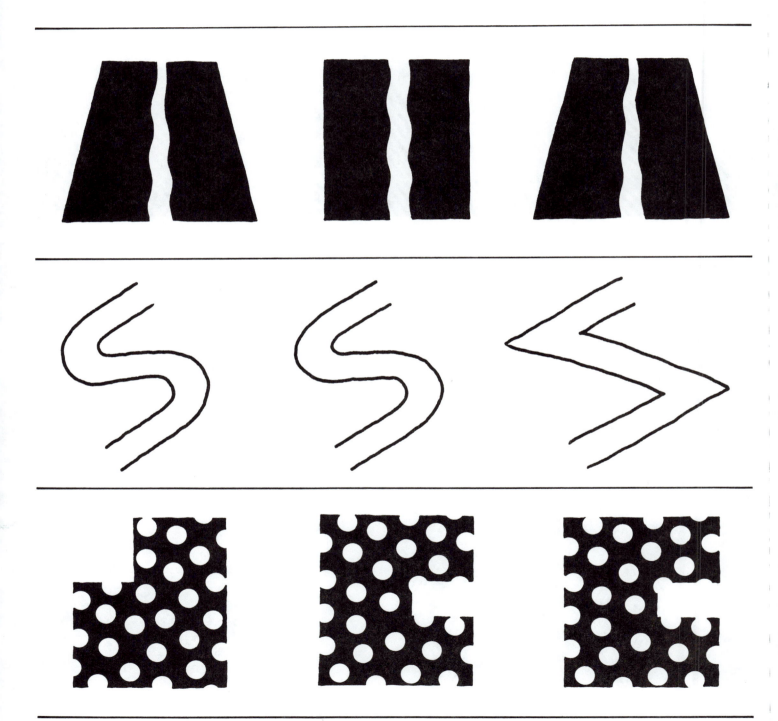

Circle the letters that are **different**.

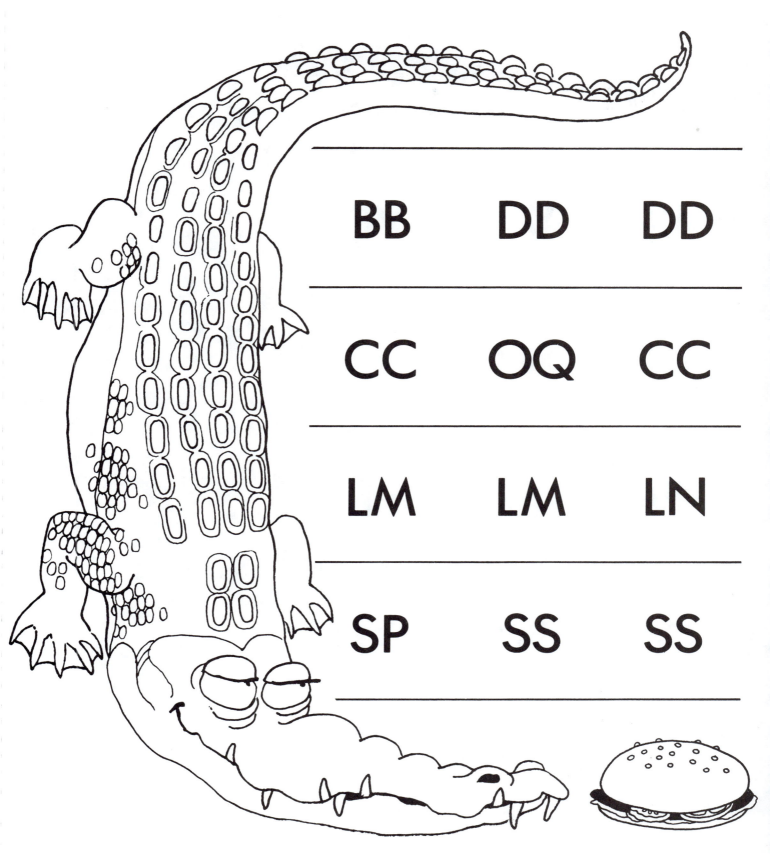

BB   DD   DD

CC   OQ   CC

LM   LM   LN

SP   SS   SS

Circle the letters that are **different**.

YE   VY   YE

IJ   JJ   JJ

FF   FF   FE

GH   GA   GH

Circle the letters that are **different**.

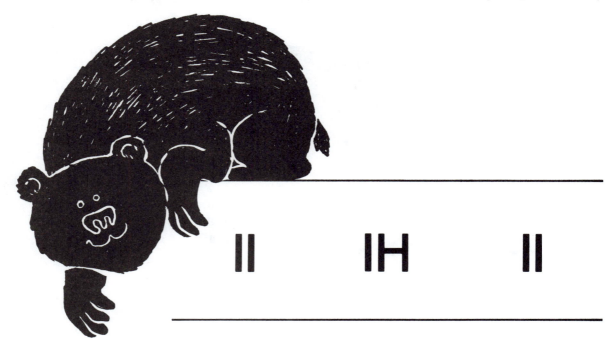

II IH II

MN MN NN

UJ VJ VJ

AZ AN AZ

Circle the word that is **different**.

GO   GO   IF

DOG   DID   DOG

ALL   ALL   BUT

WHO   SHE   WHO

64

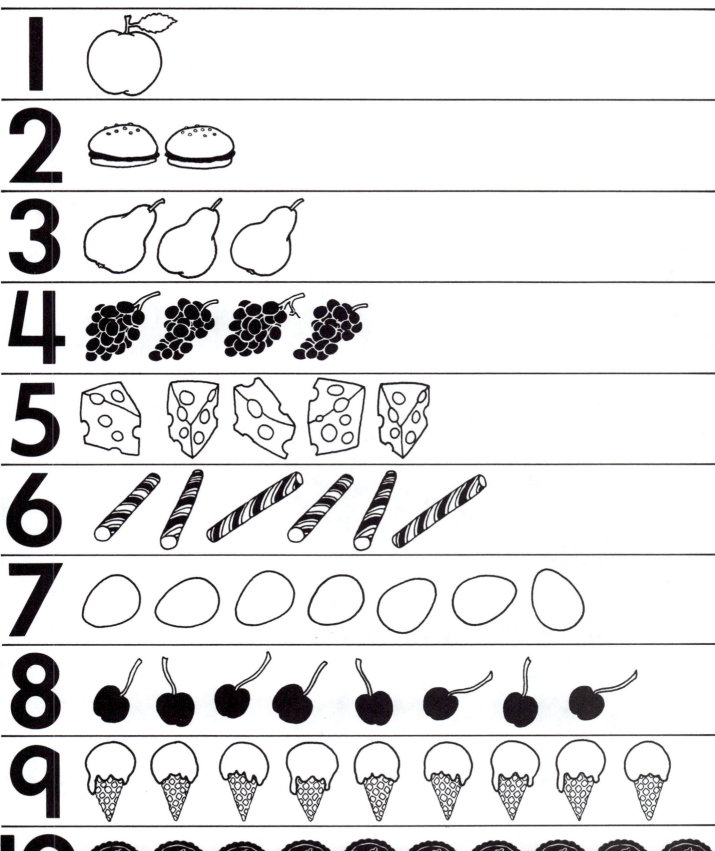

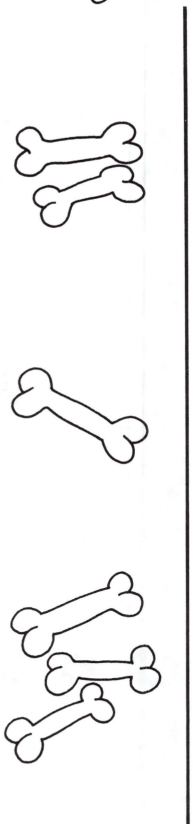

I

one

There is **1** of something. Circle the **1** thing.

Trace **1**. Then write **1**.

2 two

Circle **2** .

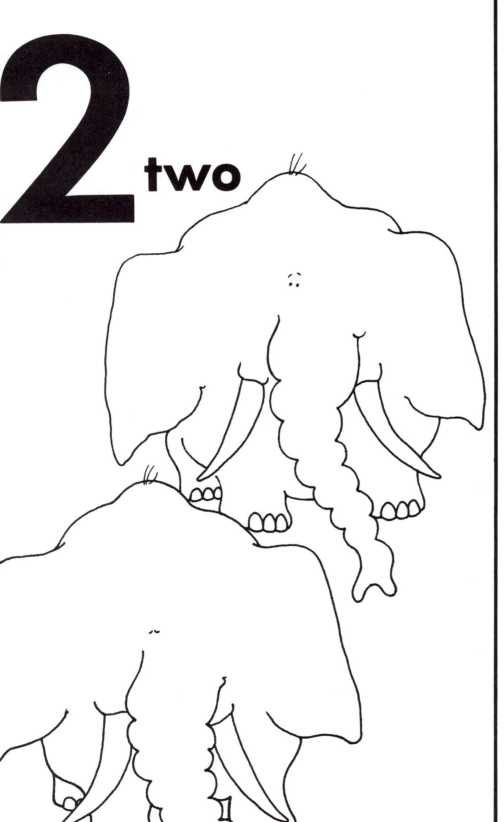

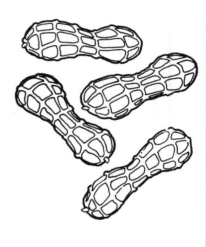

68

There are **2** of something. Circle the group of **2**.

Trace **2**. Then write **2**.

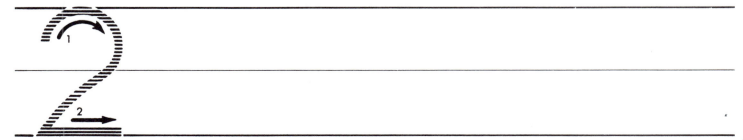

3 three

Circle **3** .

There are **3** of something. Circle the group of **3**. ▬▬▬

Trace **3**. Then write **3**. ▬▬▬

4 four

72

There are **4** of something. Circle the group of **4.** ▄▄▄▄▄▄

Trace **4.** Then write **4.** ◀▬▬▬▬▬▬▬▶▬▬▬▬▬

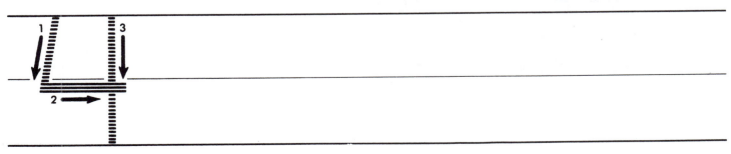

5 five

Circle 5

There are **5** of something. Circle the group of 5. ▬▬▬

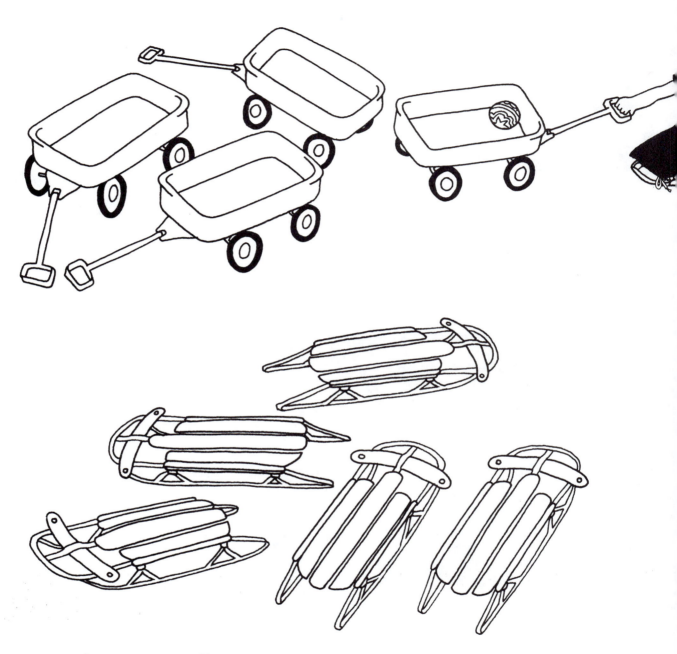

Trace **5**. Then write **5**. ▬▬▬▬▬▬

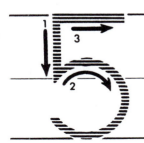

6 six

There are **6** of something. Circle the group of **6**. ▬▬▬

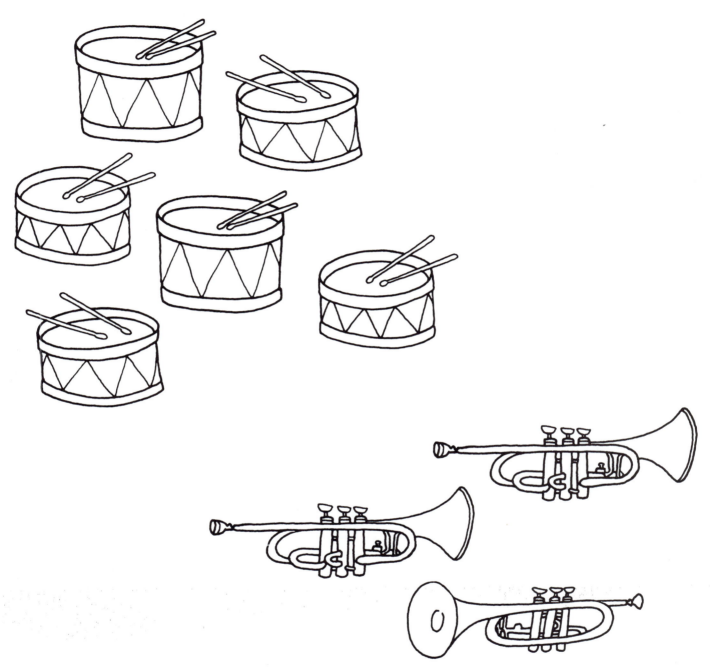

Trace **6**. Then write **6**. ▬▬▬▬▬▬▬

7 seven

78

There are **7** of something. Circle the group of **7.** ▬▬

Trace **7**. Then write **7.** ▬▬▬▬▬

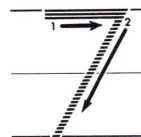

8 eight

There are **8** of something. Circle the group of **8**.

Trace **8**. Then write **8**.

9 nine

82

There are 9 of something. Circle the group of 9. ▬▬▬▬▬

Trace 9. Then write 9. ▬▬▬▬▬▬▬▬▬▬▬▬

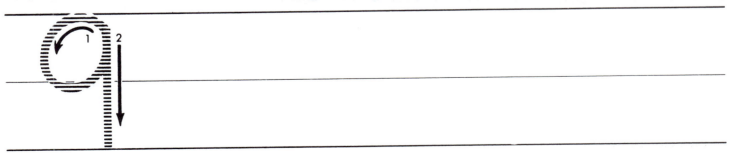

10 ten

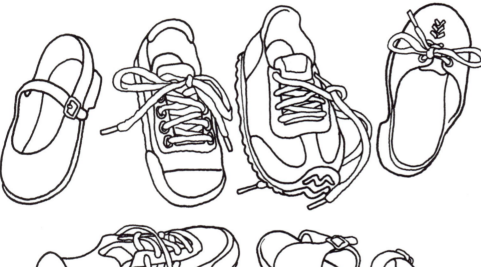

There are **10** of something. Circle the group of **10.** ━━━━

Trace **10.** Then write **10.** ━━━━━━

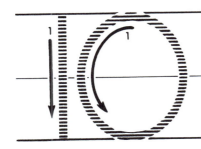

Trace the number. Then write it.

Trace the number. Then write it.

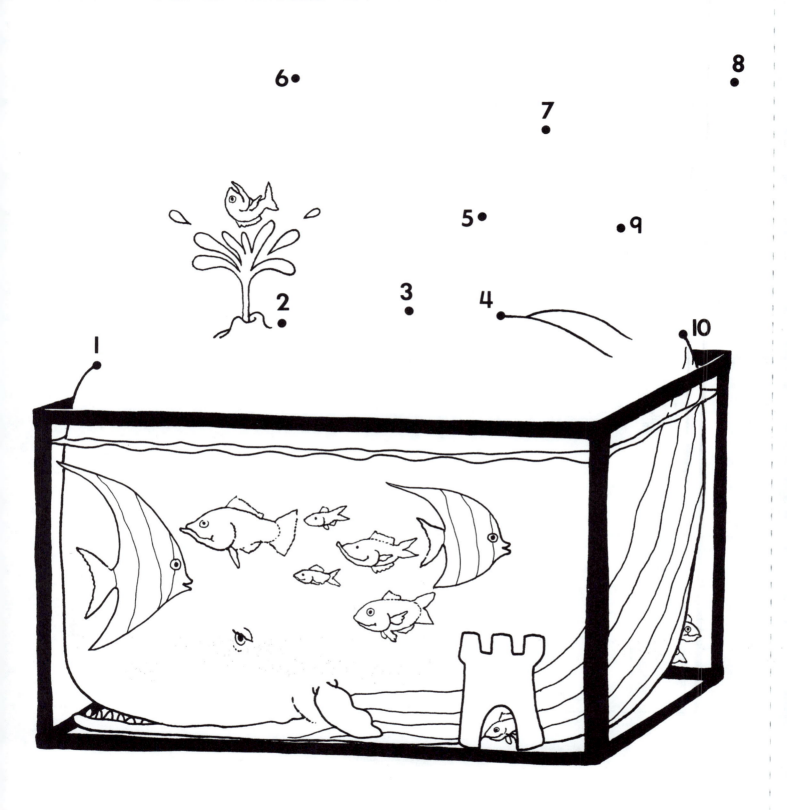

Connect the dots from **1** to **10.**

8   9   10

3   4   5

5   6   7

7   8   9

Circle the correct number.

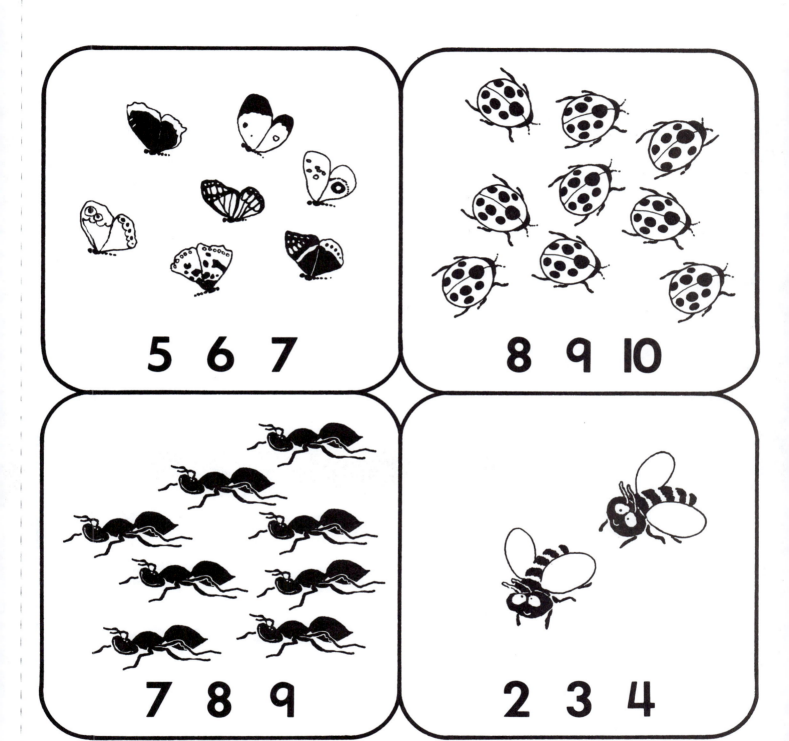

5 6 7

8 9 10

7 8 9

2 3 4

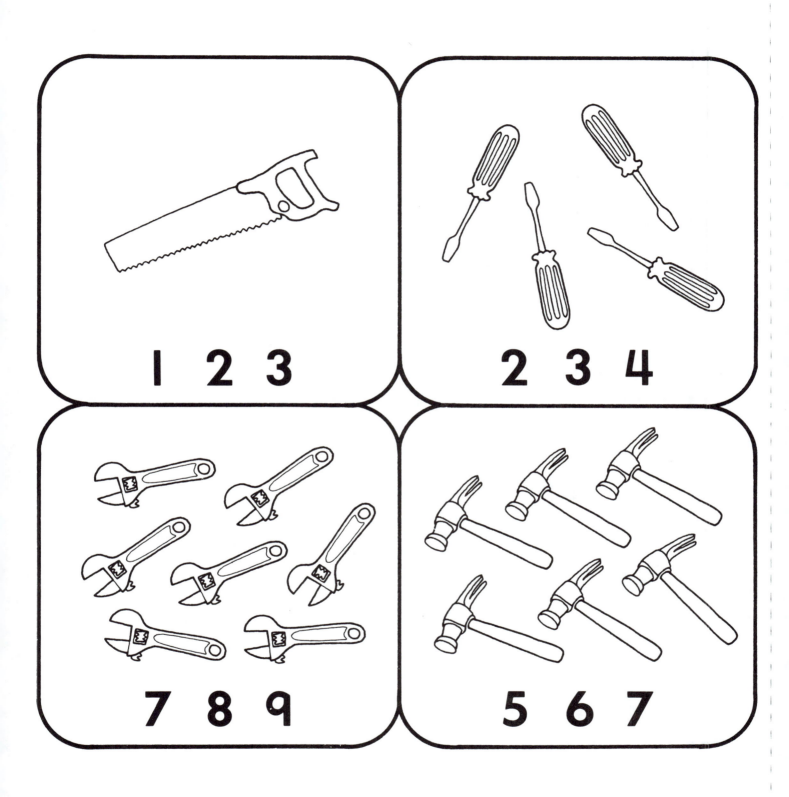

1   2   3

2   3   4

7   8   9

5   6   7

Read the word.

three	2	4	3	10
five	5	7	4	6
seven	2	10	7	1
one	1	2	10	6
six	8	6	5	9

Circle the number that is the same as the word.

ten	6	10	7	8
eight	1	2	8	9
four	3	4	6	8
two	4	3	2	9
nine	5	1	7	9

Circle the number that is the same as the word.

Write the correct number on the line.

How many 🏠 ? _____

How many 🐔 ? _____

How many 🐑 ? _____

Write the correct number on the line.

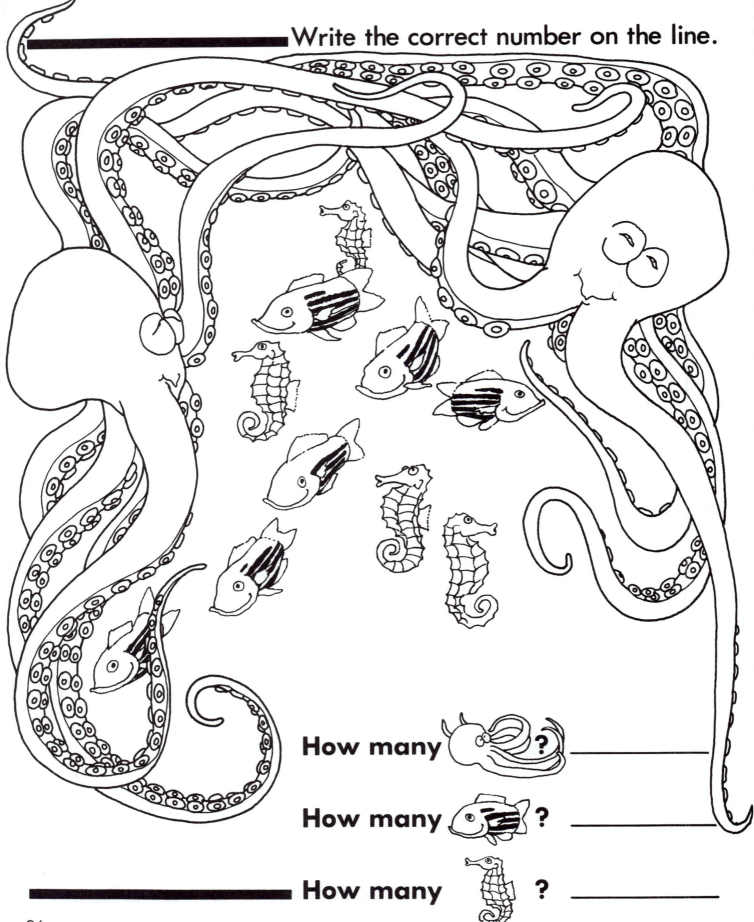

How many ? _____

How many ? _____

How many ? _____

SKY HIGH

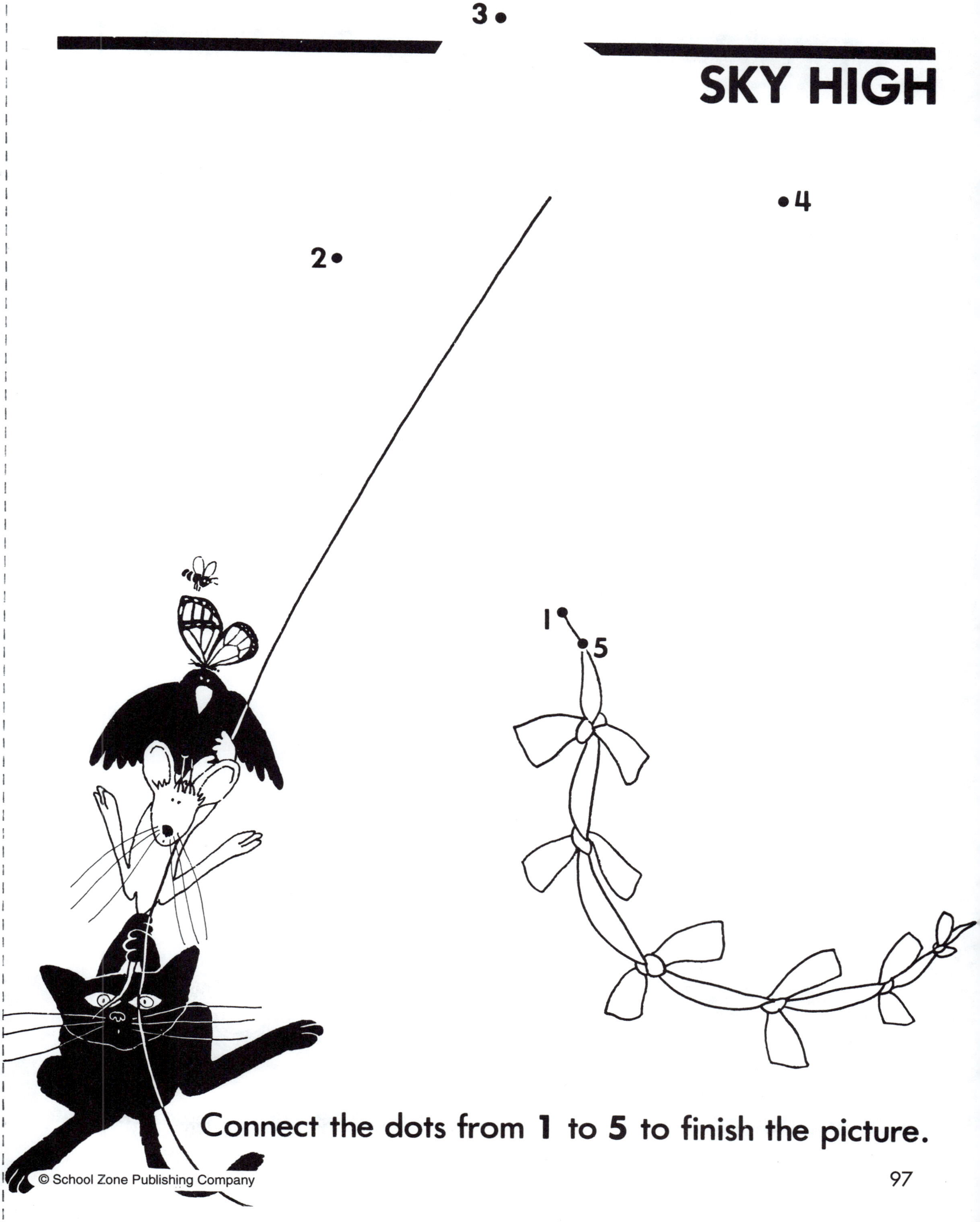

●4

2●

1●
●5

Connect the dots from 1 to 5 to finish the picture.

SO TALL!

2• •3

•4

1• •5

Connect the dots from **1** to **5** to finish the picture.

A NEW FRIEND

Connect the dots from **1** to **5** to finish the picture.

WHERE IS CARLA?

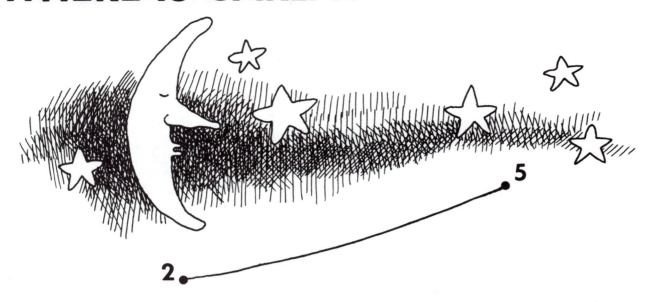

Connect the dots from 1 to 5 to finish the picture.

STAND ASIDE!

Connect the dots from **1** to **5** to finish the picture.

RUN, MOUSE, RUN!

Connect the dots from 1 to 8 to finish the picture.

A SCARY CASTLE!

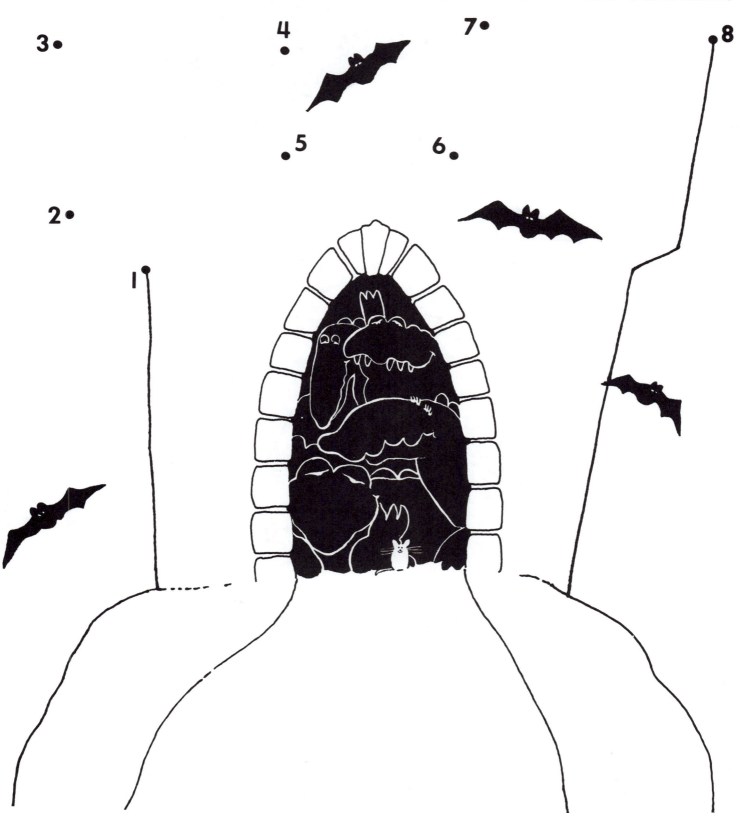

Connect the dots from 1 to 8 to finish the picture.

103

WHAT'S NEW?

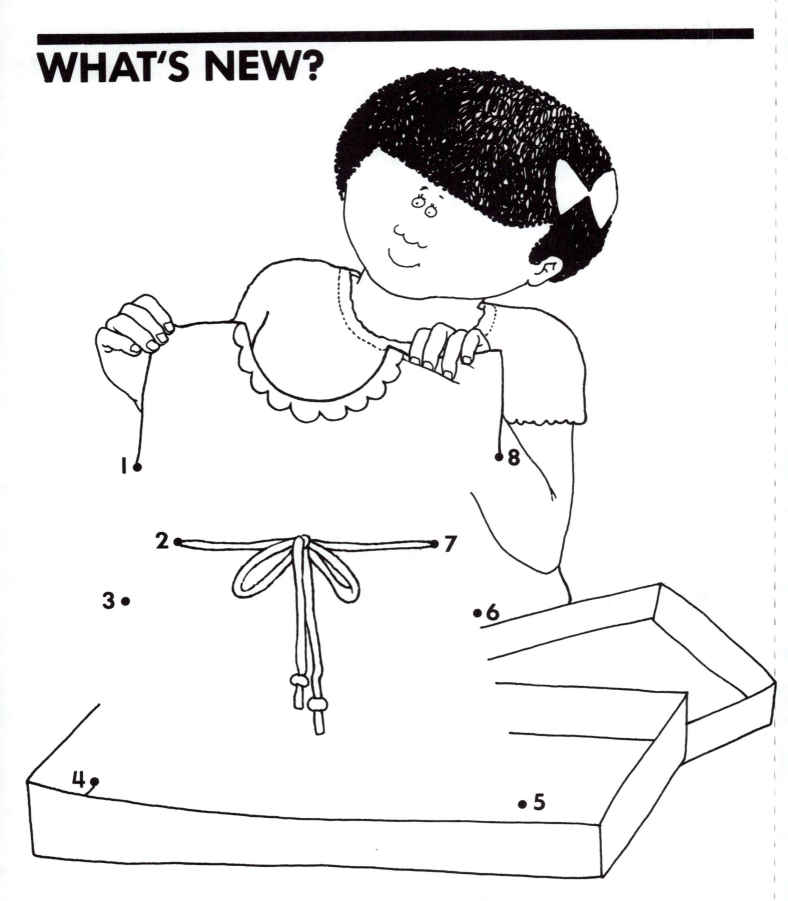

Connect the dots from 1 to 8 to finish the picture.

WHERE IS KING?

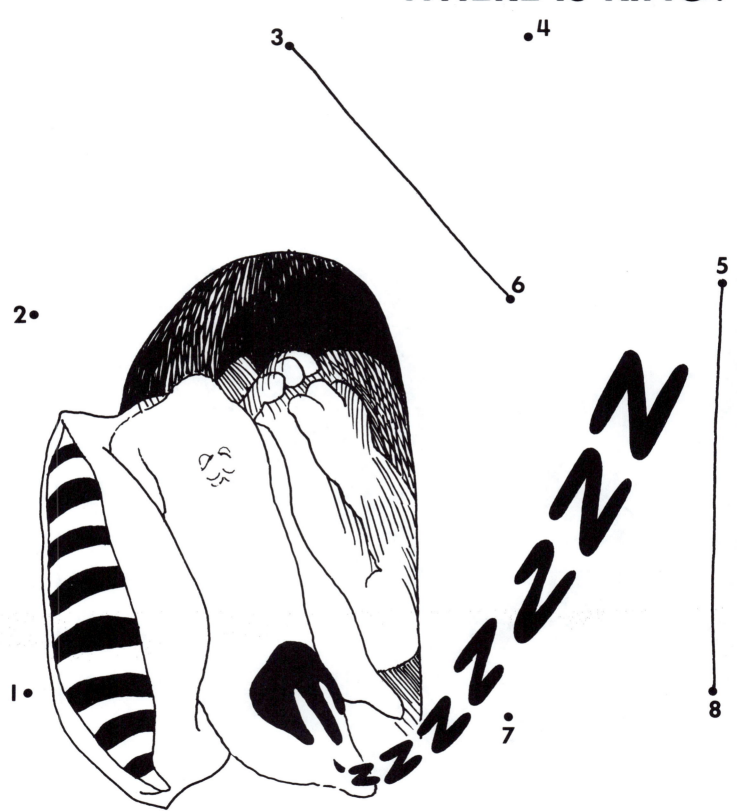

Connect the dots from **1** to **8** to finish the picture.

LOOK OUT BELOW!

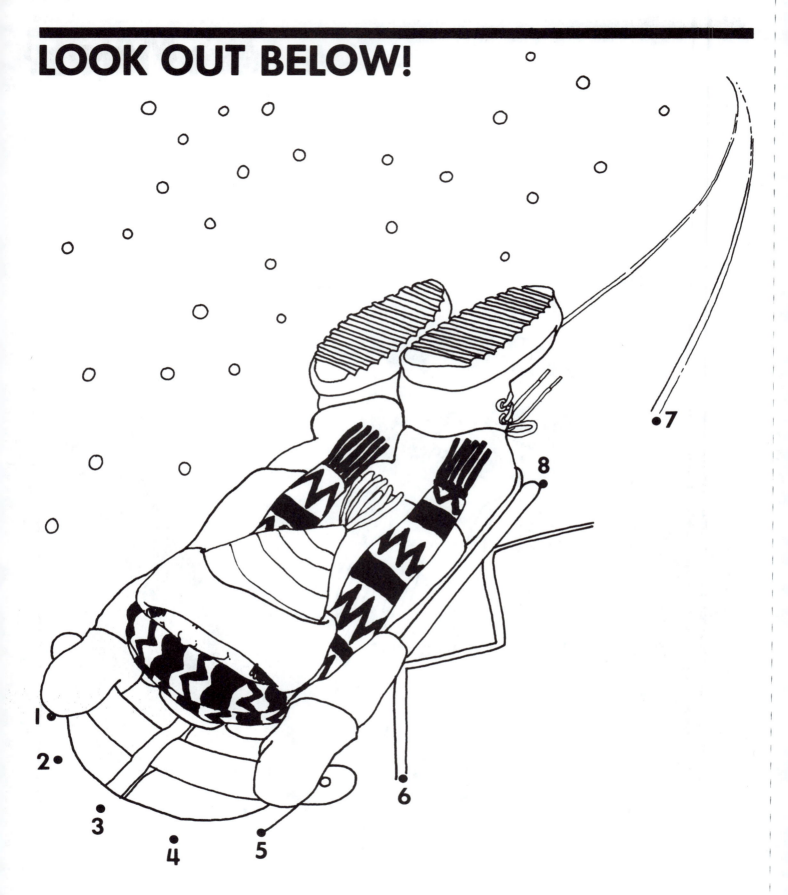

Connect the dots from **1** to **8** to finish the picture.

IT'S MAGIC!

Connect the dots from 1 to 8 to finish the picture.

WHERE ARE SARAH AND JASON?

5

3

4

6

7

2•

8

1•

Connect the dots from **1** to **8** to finish the picture.

FISH, FISH, FISH!

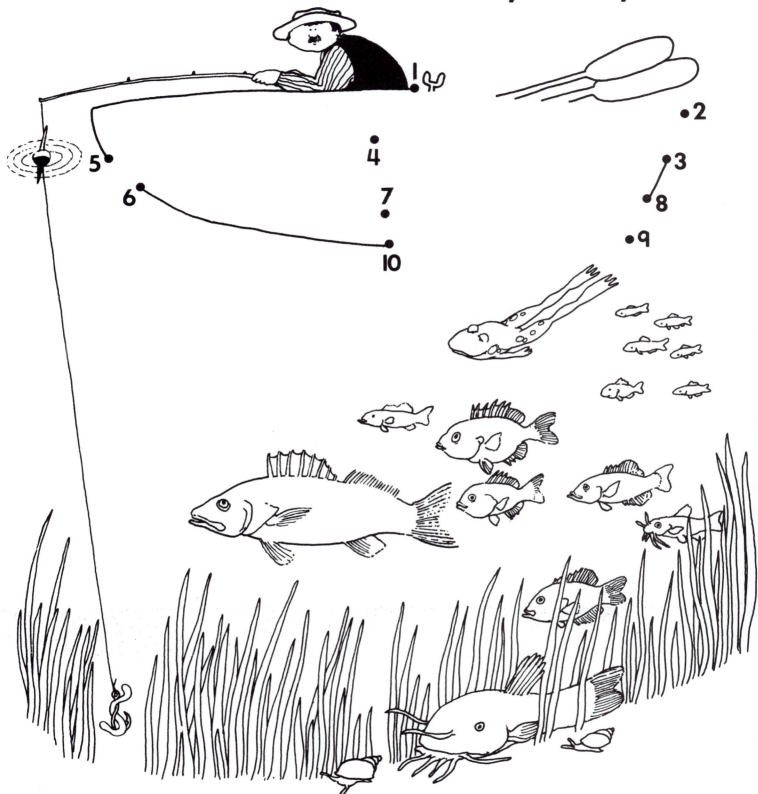

Connect the dots from 1 to 10 to finish the picture.

SLEEPY TIME

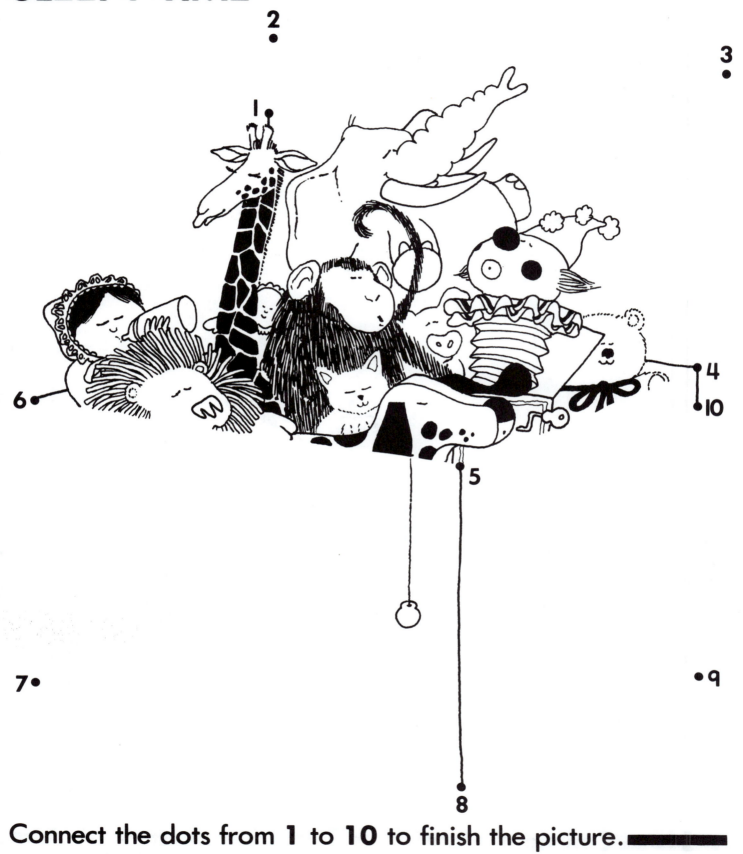

Connect the dots from **1** to **10** to finish the picture.

LOOK OUT BELOW!

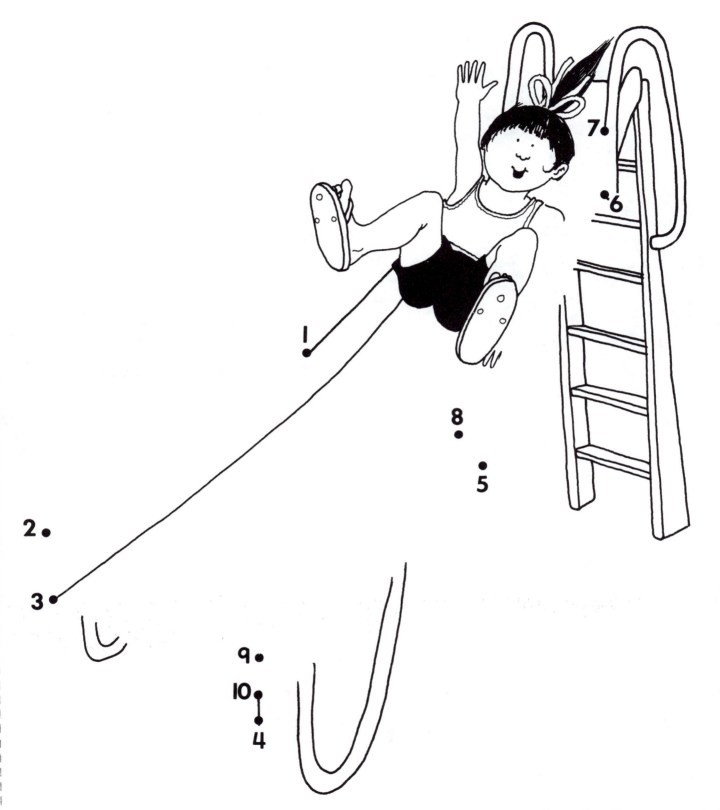

Connect the dots from **1** to **10** to finish the picture.

111

WHAT DID BABY BEAR FIND?

Connect the dots from 1 to 10 to finish the picture. ▬▬

WHERE IS MONKEY?

Connect the dots from 1 to 10 to finish the picture.

114

WHAT A LOAD

Connect the dots from **1** to **10** to finish the picture.

WHERE IS TERRY?

Connect the dots from 1 to 10 to finish the picture.

Connect the dots from 1 to 10 to finish the picture.

WHAT IS STEVE DOING?

Connect the dots from 1 to 10 to finish the picture.

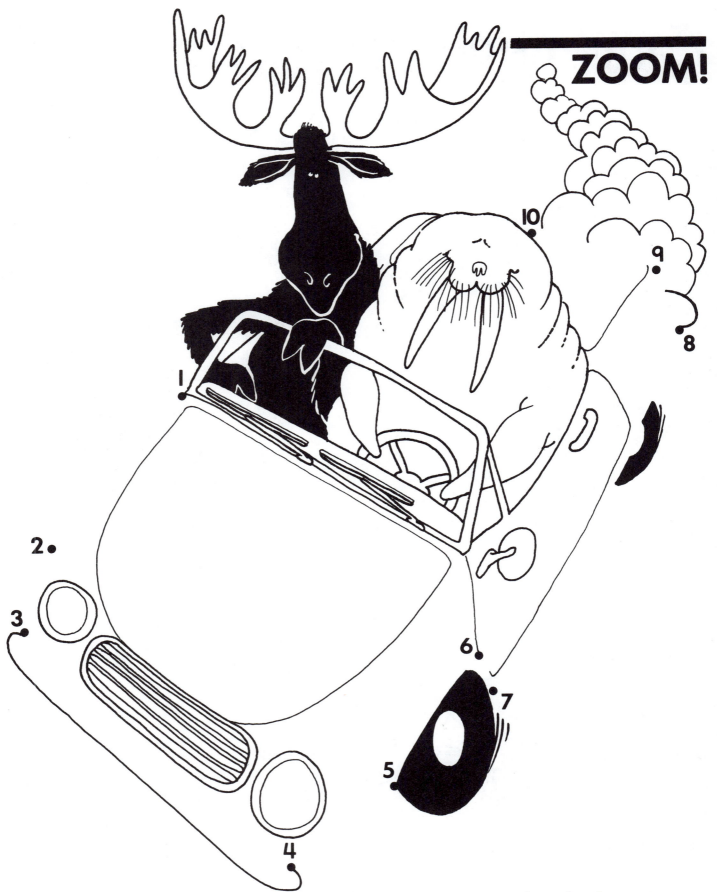

ZOOM!

Connect the dots from **1** to **10** to finish the picture.

119

CHUG, CHUG

Connect the dots from 1 to 10 to finish the picture.

120

LET ME HELP YOU

Connect the dots from 1 to 10 to finish the picture.

121

WHAT'S THAT!

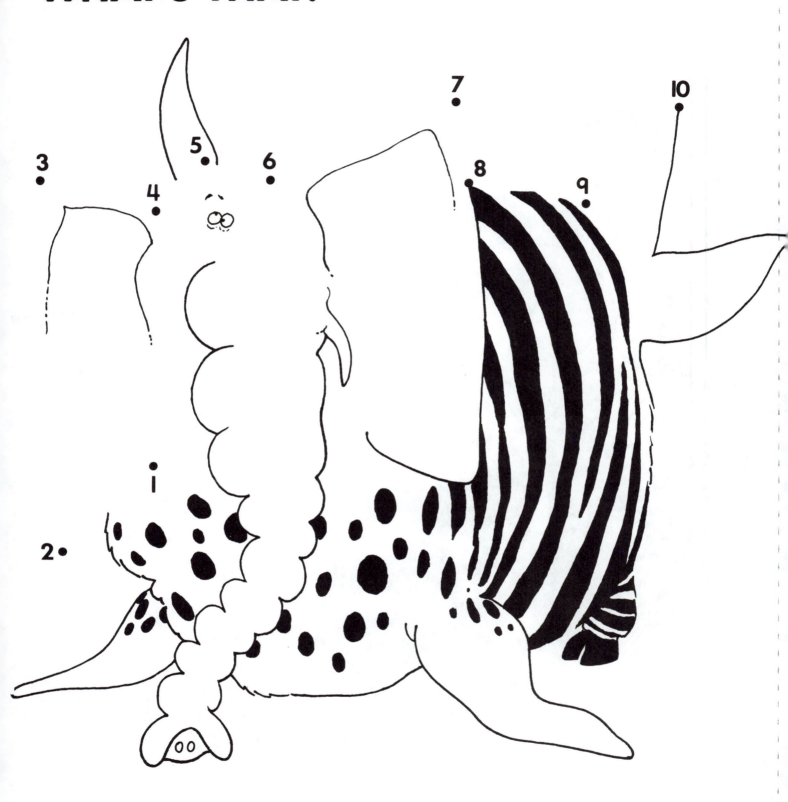

Connect the dots from **1** to **10** to finish the picture.

TURTLE'S HOME

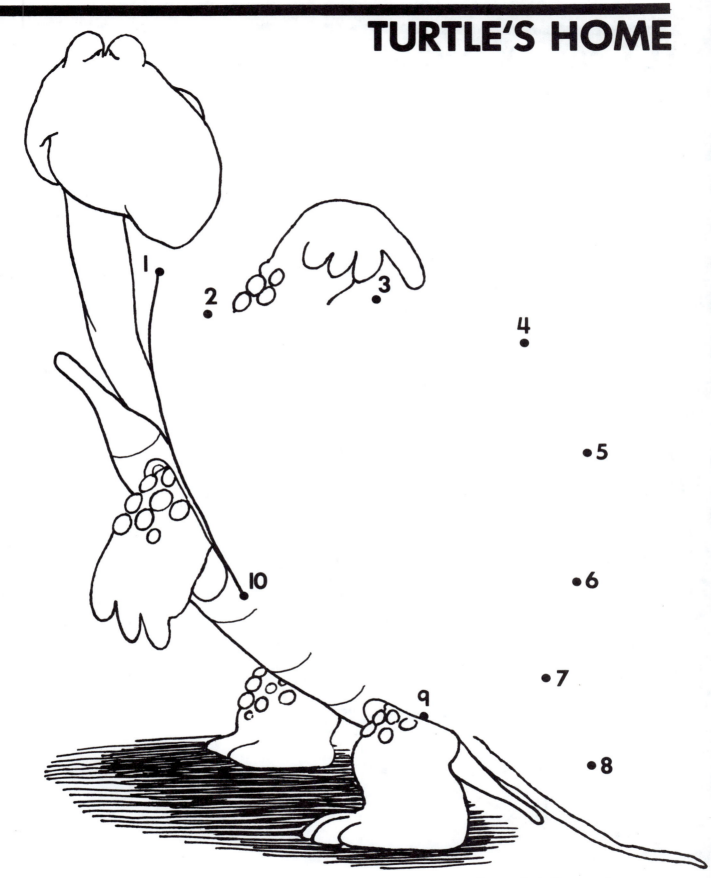

Connect the dots from **1** to **10** to finish the picture.

123

LET ME DOWN!

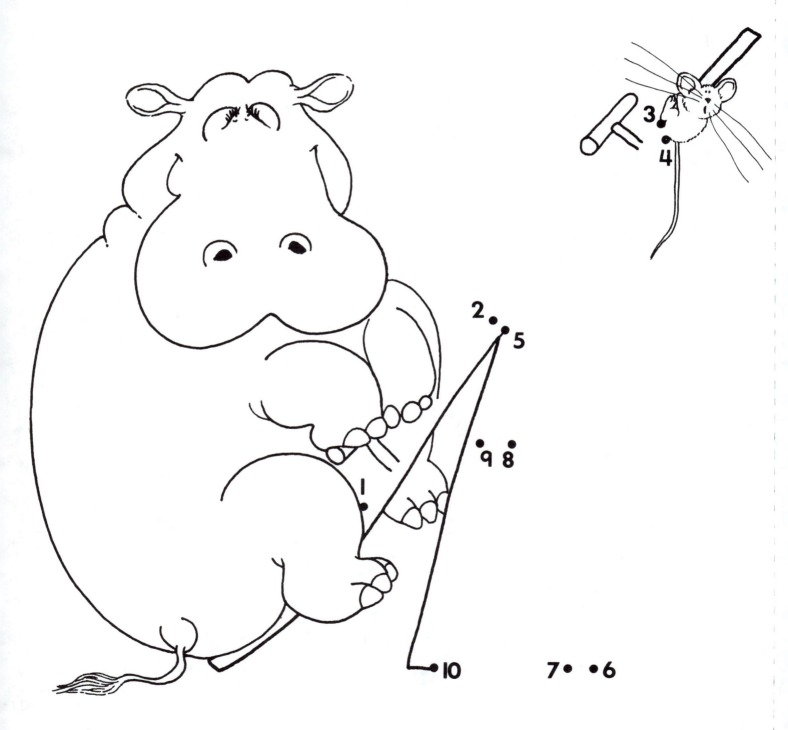

Connect the dots from 1 to 10 to finish the picture.

WHOSE FACE?

Connect the dots from **1** to **10** to finish the picture.

HELP!

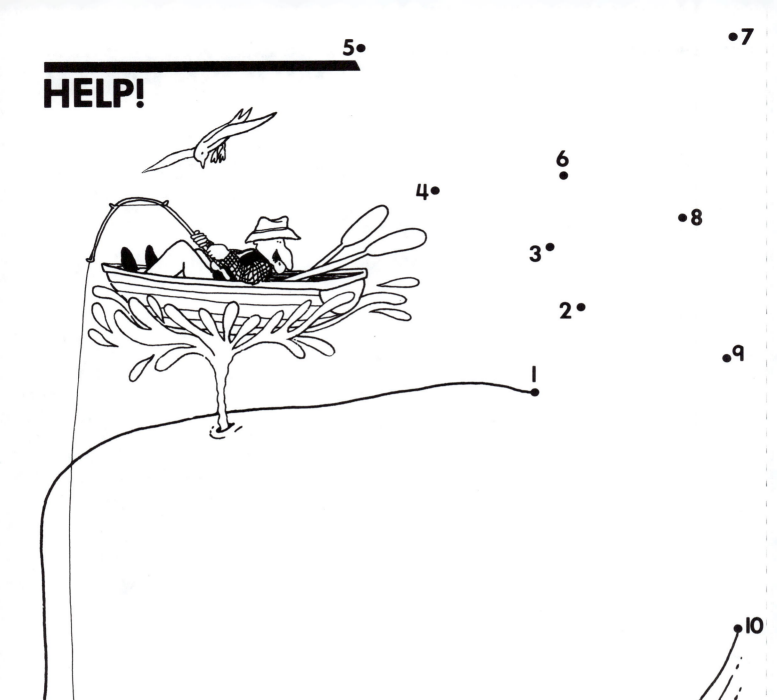

Connect the dots from **1** to **10** to finish the picture.

Connect the dots from 1 to 10 to finish the picture.

OOPS!

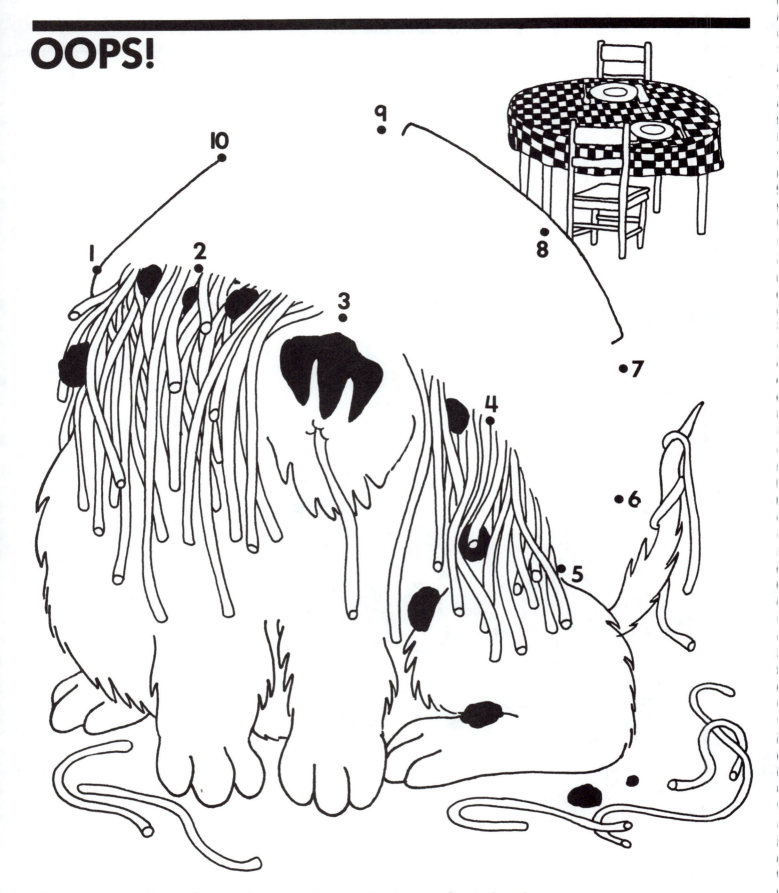

Connect the dots from 1 to 10 to finish the picture.

SQUARE

This is a **square**.

Circle the **2** shapes.

SQUARE

This is a **square**. Color the ☐ .

Circle the **2** ☐ shapes.

130

Circle the thing that has a ⬜ **shape.**

SQUARE

Trace the ☐ .

Make the shape a ☐ .

SQUARE

Circle the ☐ shapes in the picture.

133

RECTANGLE

This is a **rectangle**.

Circle the **2**  shapes.

RECTANGLE

This is a **rectangle**. Color the ▭ .

Circle the **2** ▭ shapes.

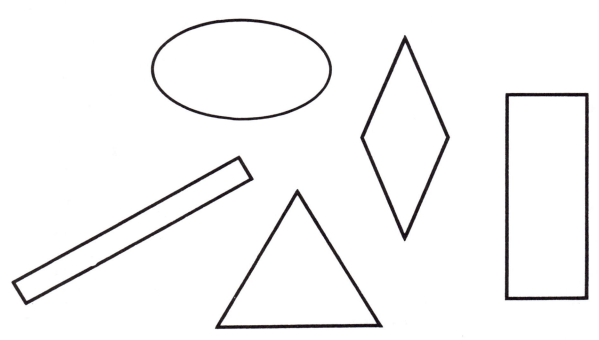

RECTANGLE

Circle the thing that has a ⬜ shape.

Trace the ☐ .

Make the shape a ☐ .

RECTANGLE

Circle the ⬚ shapes in the picture.

This is a **triangle**.

Circle the **2** 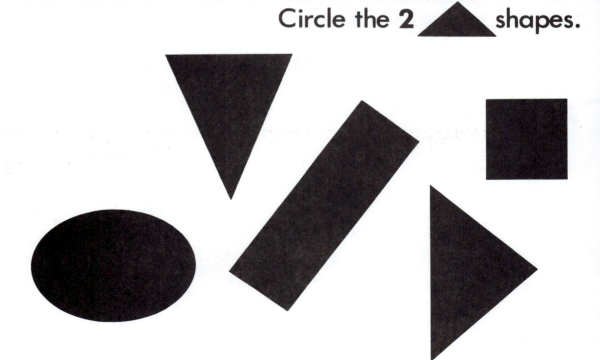 shapes.

TRIANGLE

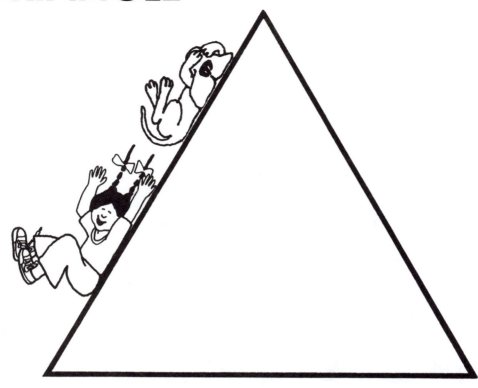

This is a **triangle**. Color the △.

Circle the **2** △ shapes.

140

Circle the thing that has a △ shape.

TRIANGLE

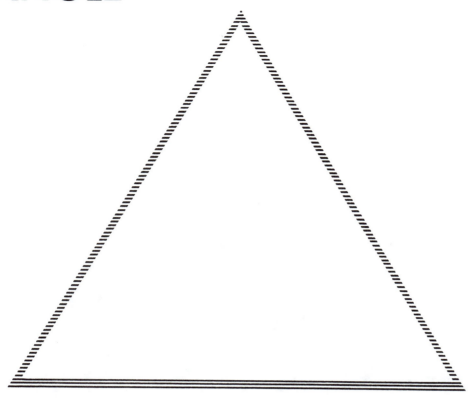

Trace the △.

Make the shape a △.

TRIANGLE

Circle the △ shapes in the picture.

CIRCLE

This is a **circle**.

Circle the **2** ● shapes.

CIRCLE

This is a **circle**. Color the .

Circle the **2** shapes.

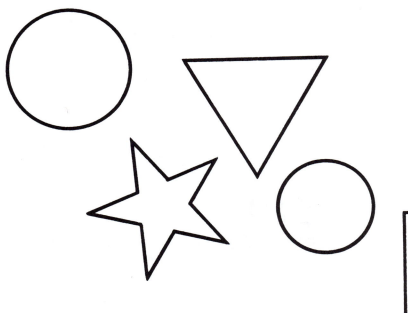

145

CIRCLE

Circle the thing that has a ⭘ shape.

CIRCLE

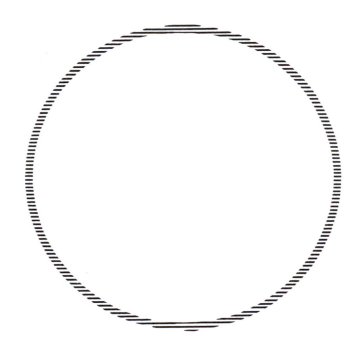

Trace the .

Make the shape a .

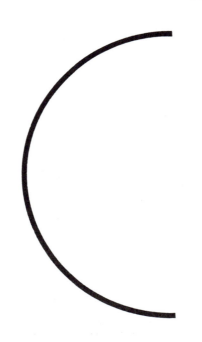

CIRCLE

Circle the ◯ shapes in the picture.

This is an **oval**.

Circle the **2**  shapes.

OVAL

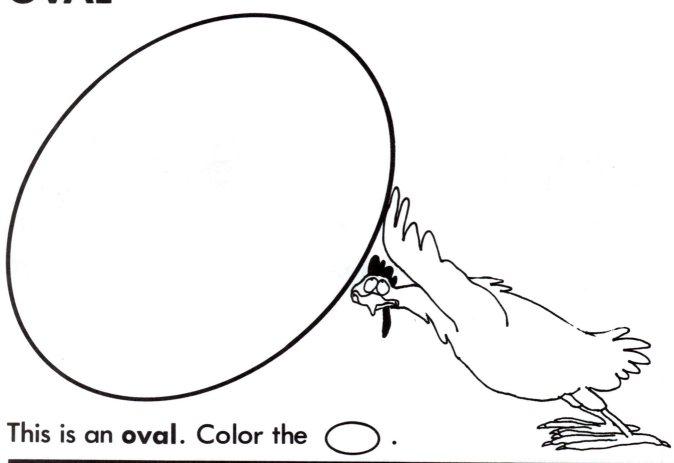

This is an **oval**. Color the ⬭ .

Circle the **2** ⬭ shapes.

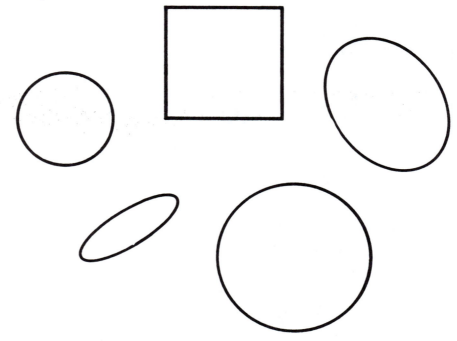

150

Circle the thing that has an ⬭ shape.

OVAL

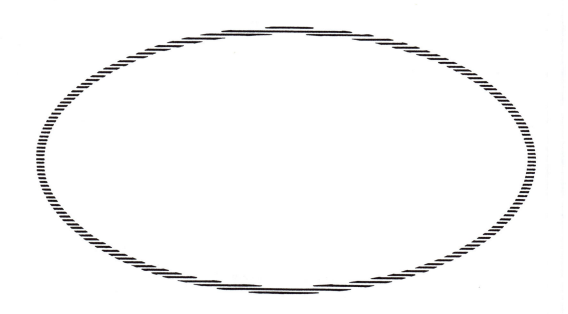

Trace the ⬭ .

Make the shape an ⬭ .

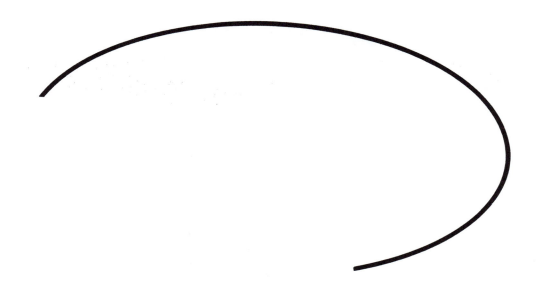

Circle the ⬭ shapes in the picture.

MATCH THE SHAPES

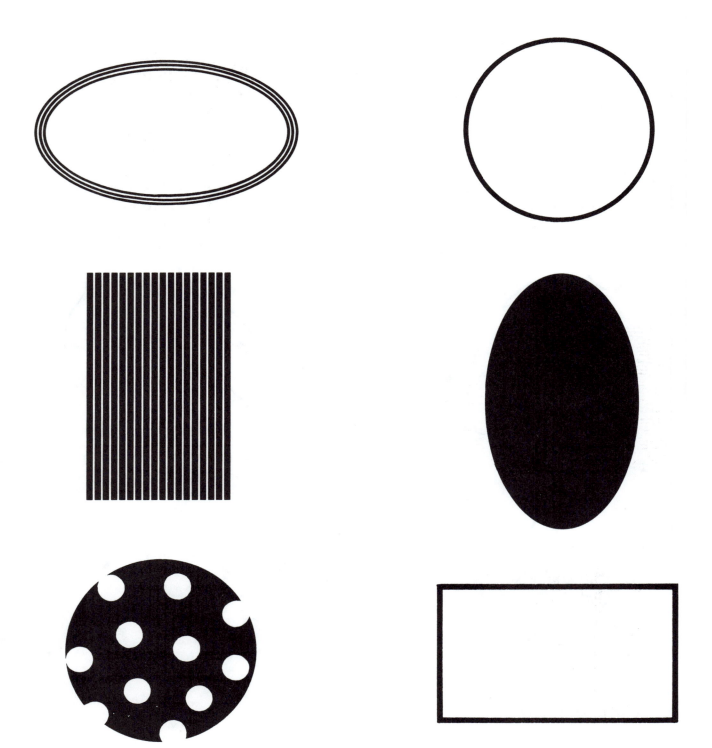

Draw lines to the shapes that have the same name.

MATCH THE SHAPES

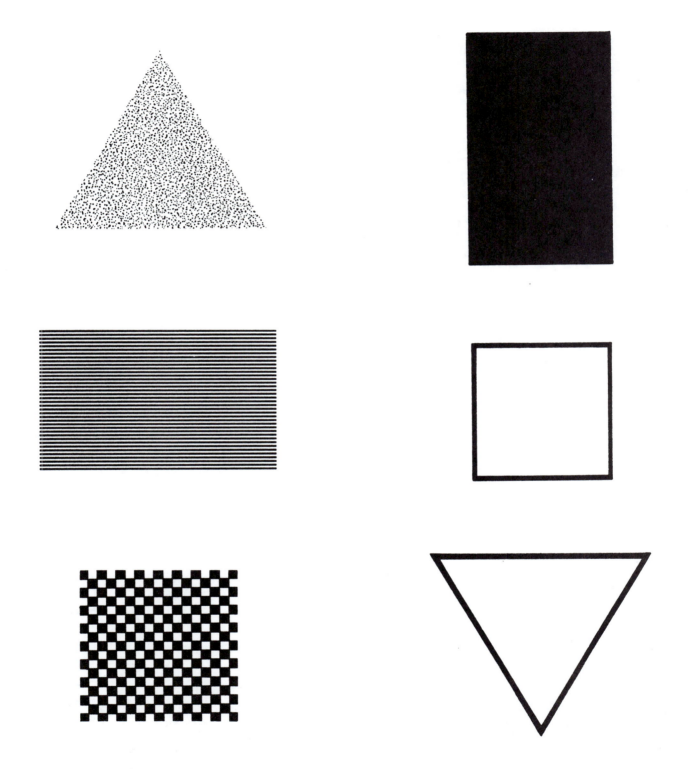

Draw lines to the shapes that have the same name.

COLOR THE SHAPES

Color all the ◯ shapes one color.

Color all the ▭ shapes another color.

COLOR THE SHAPES

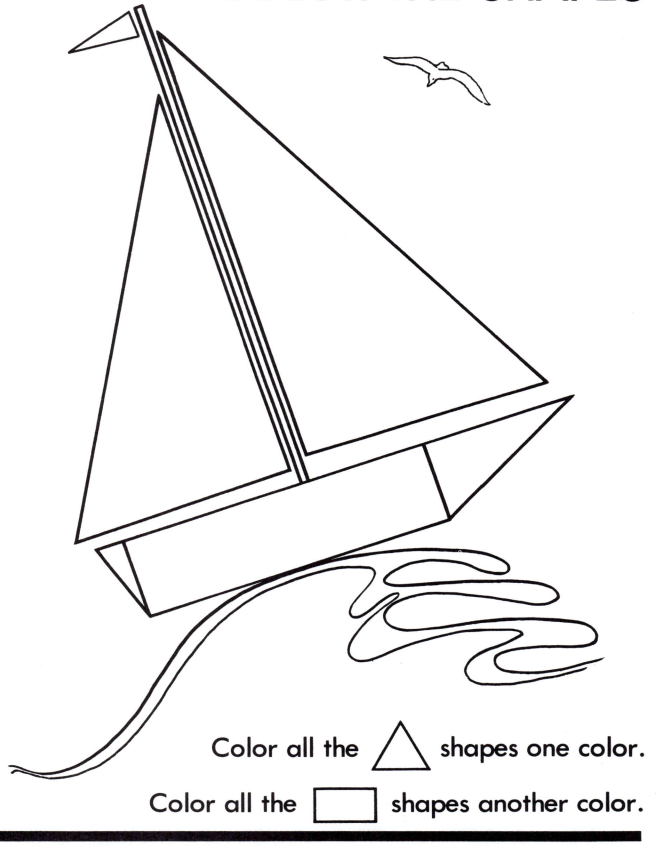

Color all the △ shapes one color.

Color all the ▭ shapes another color.

COLOR THE SHAPES

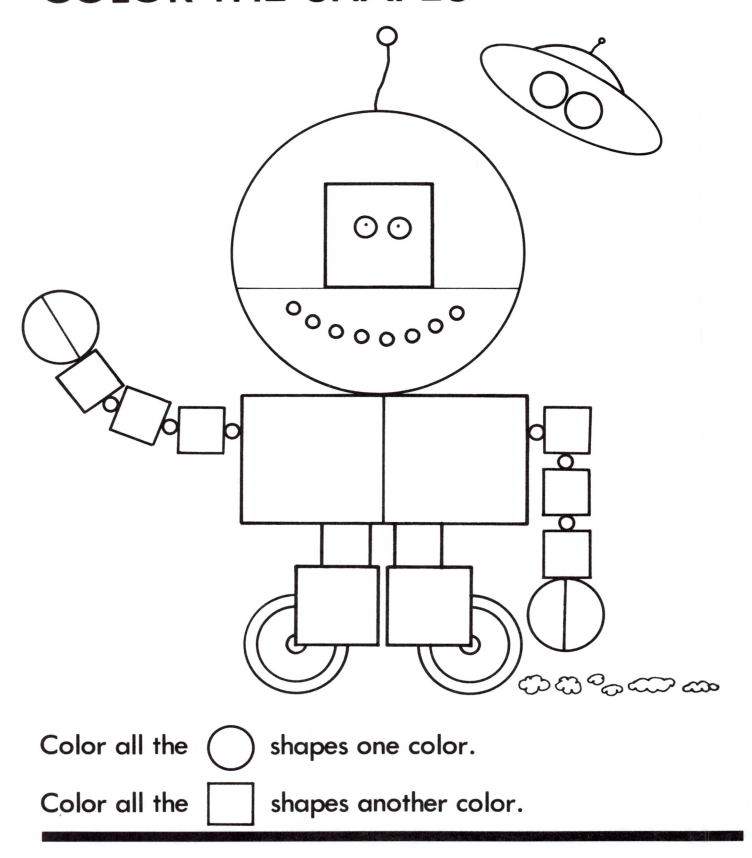

Color all the ⬭ shapes one color.

Color all the ☐ shapes another color.

DRAW THE SHAPES

Trace the □ . Then draw a □ .

Trace the ○ . Then draw a ○ .

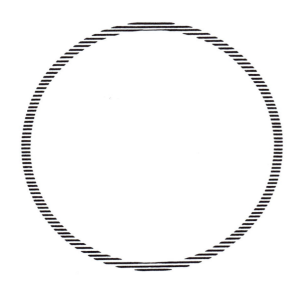

DRAW THE SHAPES

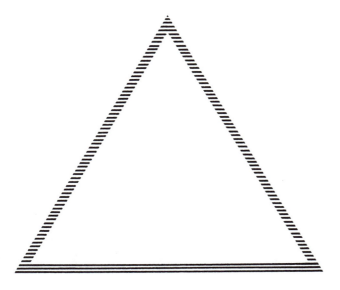

Trace the △ . Then draw a △ .

Trace the ▭ . Then draw a ▭ .

Help the gopher
get to her den.

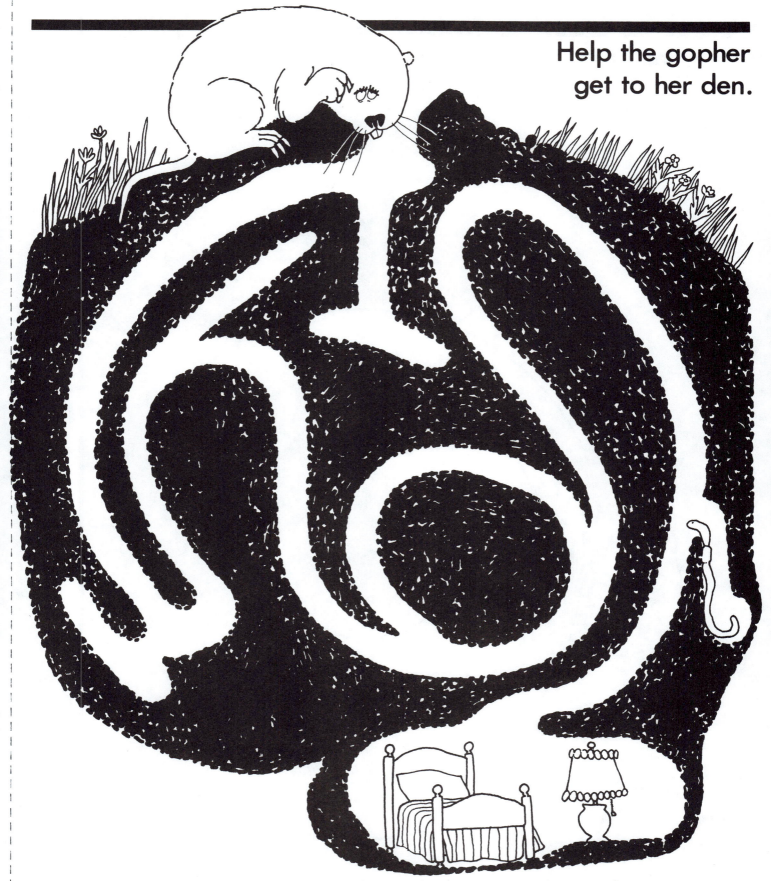

Draw a line that shows how she must go.

Help the farmer find his tractor.

Draw a line that shows how he must go.

Help the spaceman get back to Earth.

Draw a line that shows how he must go.

Help the fireman get to the truck.

Draw a line that shows how he must go.

Help the rabbit find his home.

Draw a line that shows how he must go.

Help the swimmer get to the end of the pool.

Draw a line that shows how she must go.

Help the ant get out of the ground.

Draw a line that shows how it must go.

Becky wants to find the hidden Easter Egg.

Draw a line that shows how she must go.

Ted wants to get to the bottom of the hill first.

Draw a line that shows how he must go.

Help Giraffe find some leaves to eat.

Draw a line that shows how he must go.

Help the pilot get to land.

Draw a line that shows how he must go.

Help the mailman deliver the mail.

Draw a line that shows how he must go.

Help Cindy and Mindy find their way to school.

Draw a line that shows how they must go.

Dinosaur wants to get to the land.

Draw a line that shows how he must go.

177

Help Butterfly get to the flower.

Draw a line that shows how she must go.

Help Tom find his coat.

Draw a line that shows how he must go.

Can Bear get to the honey?

Draw a line that shows how he must go.

Help the carpenter find his hammer.

Draw a line that shows how he must go.

Mom can't find the phone.

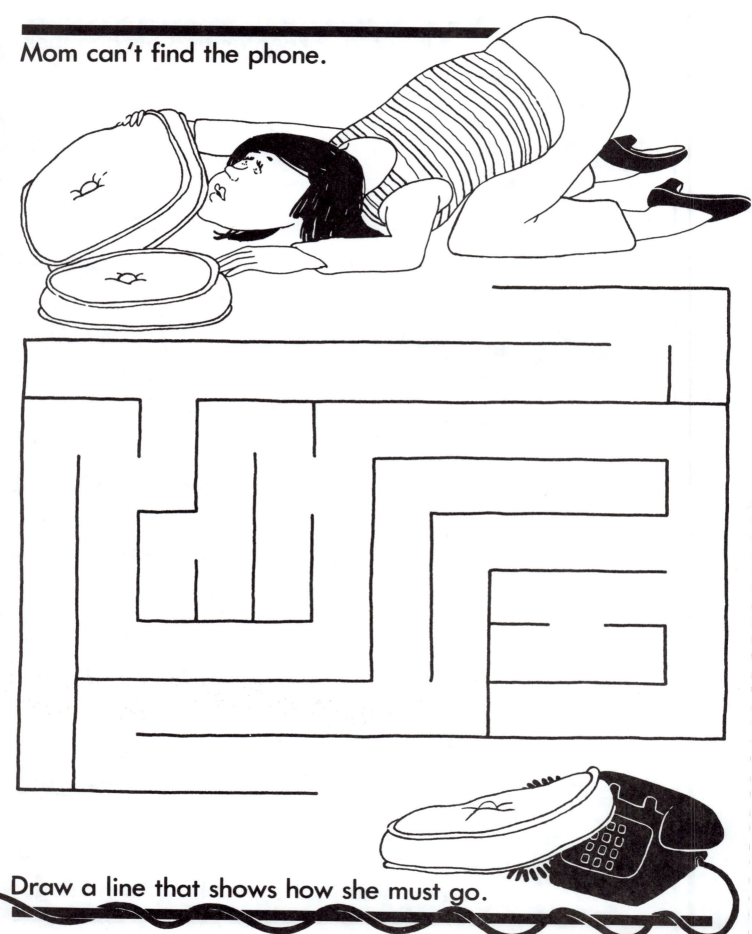

Draw a line that shows how she must go.

The boat must get to the dock.

Draw a line that shows how it must go.

Help Kevin get to the basket.

Draw a line that shows how he must go.

Help the conductor find her place.

Draw a line that shows how she must go.

Help Dad clean.

Draw a line that shows how he must go.

Help Beaver get home.

Draw a line that shows how he must go.

Help the man find the gold.

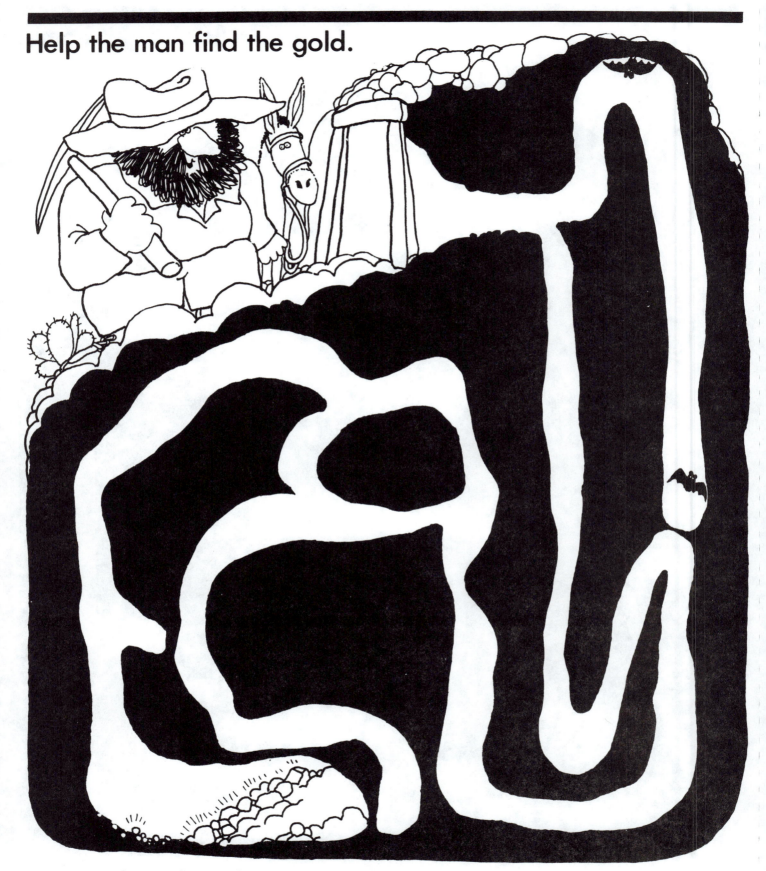

Draw a line that shows how he must go.

Help the lion tamer find the lion.

Draw a line that shows how she must go.

Help the Scotsman find his bagpipes.

Draw a line that shows how he must go.

Help the elephant find the others.

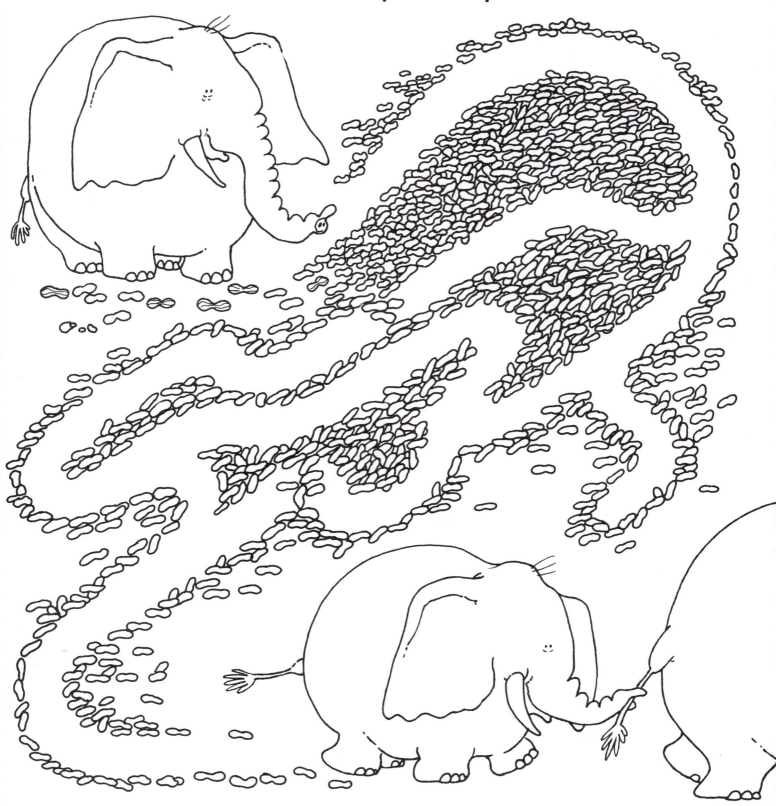

Draw a line that shows how he must go.

Help the bricklayer find his tools.

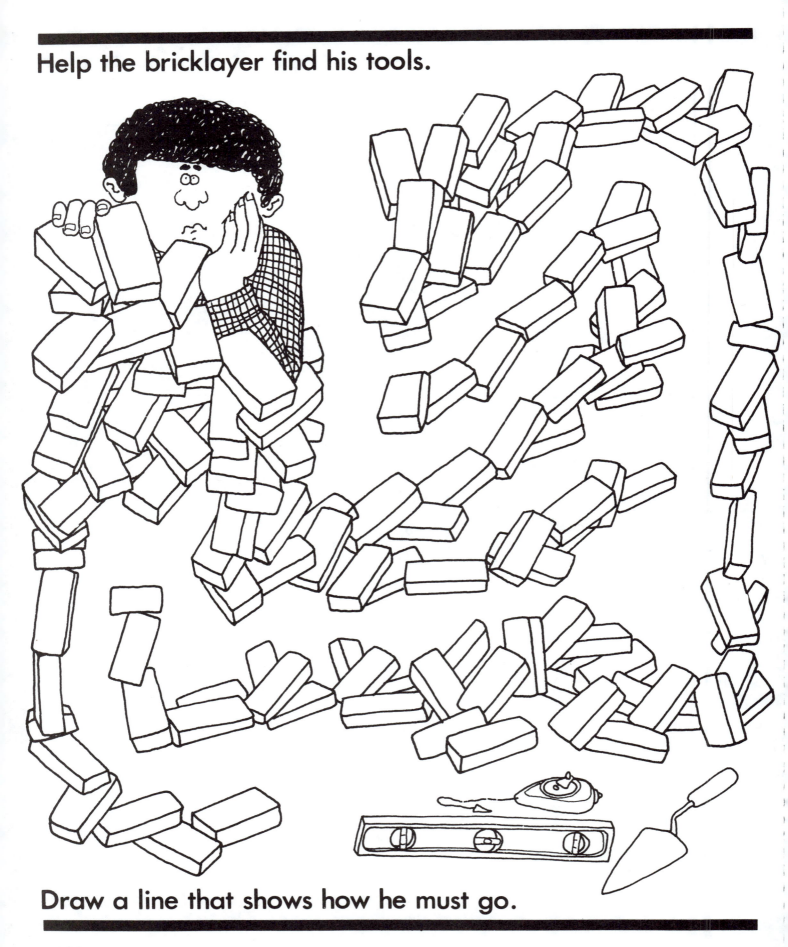

Draw a line that shows how he must go.

Peter Porcupine is on top.

Circle who is on top.

BOTTOM

Peter Porcupine is on the **bottom**.

Circle what is on the **bottom**.

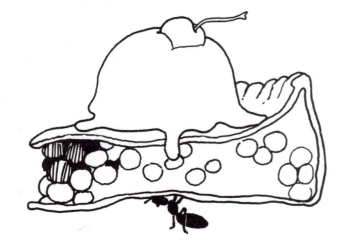

Peter Porcupine is **in** the  .

Circle who is **in** the ⊖ .

OUT

Peter Porcupine is **out** of the .

Circle who is **out** of the 🏠 .

Peter Porcupine is **on** the .

Circle what is **on** the 🪑 .

OFF

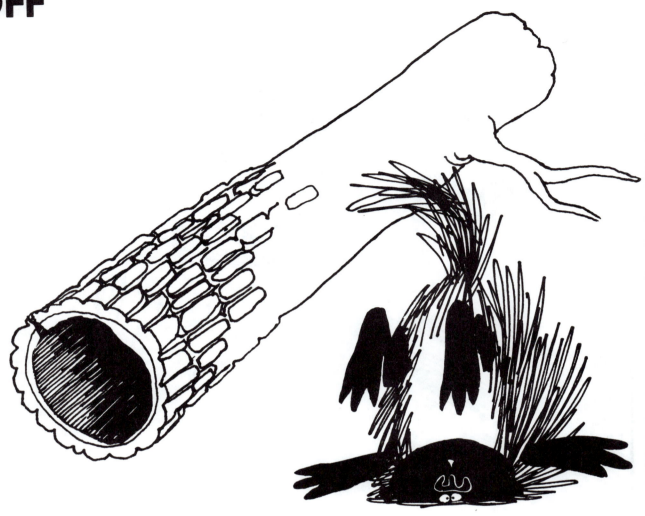

Peter Porcupine is **off** the  .

Circle what is **off** the 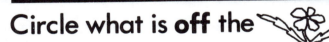 .

Peter Porcupine is **between** the 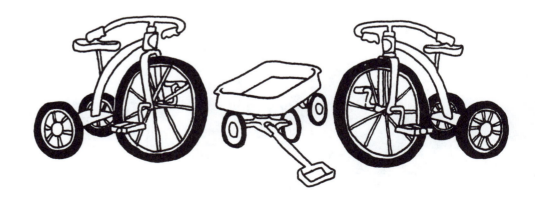.

Circle what is **between**.

BETWEEN

Peter Porcupine is **between** the and the .

Circle what is **between**.

Peter Porcupine is going **up**.

Circle what is going **up**.

DOWN

Peter Porcupine is coming **down**.

Circle what is coming **down**.

202

OVER

Peter Porcupine is going **over** the 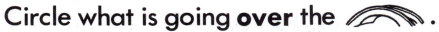.

Circle what is going **over** the .

203

UNDER

Peter Porcupine is **under** the 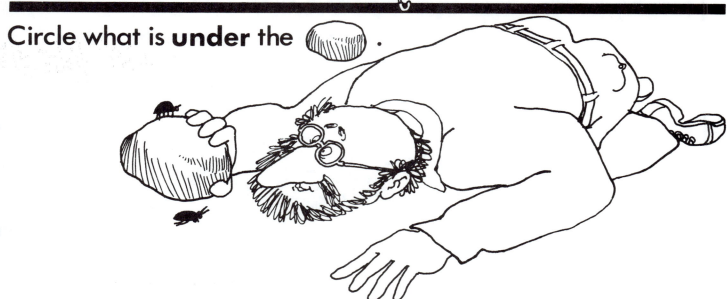.

Circle what is **under** the 🪨.

Peter Porcupine is **in front of** the  .

Circle what is **in front of** the 🏫 .

IN BACK OF

Peter Porcupine is **in back of** the .

Circle what is **in back of** the  .

206

HIGH

Peter Porcupine is **high** on the .

Circle what is **high** on the 🪜.

LOW

Peter Porcupine is **low** on the .

Circle who is **low** on the .

NEAR

Peter Porcupine is **near** the .

Circle what is **near** the  .

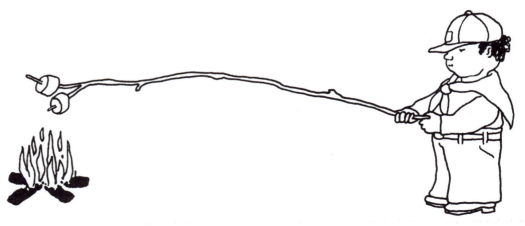

FAR

Peter Porcupine is **far** from the 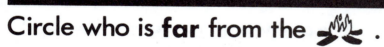.

Circle who is **far** from the 🔥.

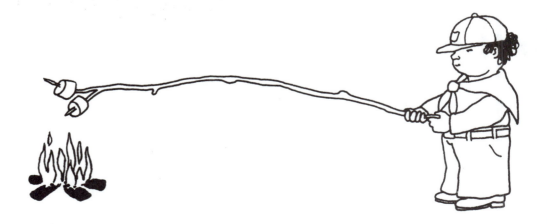

Peter Porcupine is turning **left**.

Circle what is turning **left**.

RIGHT

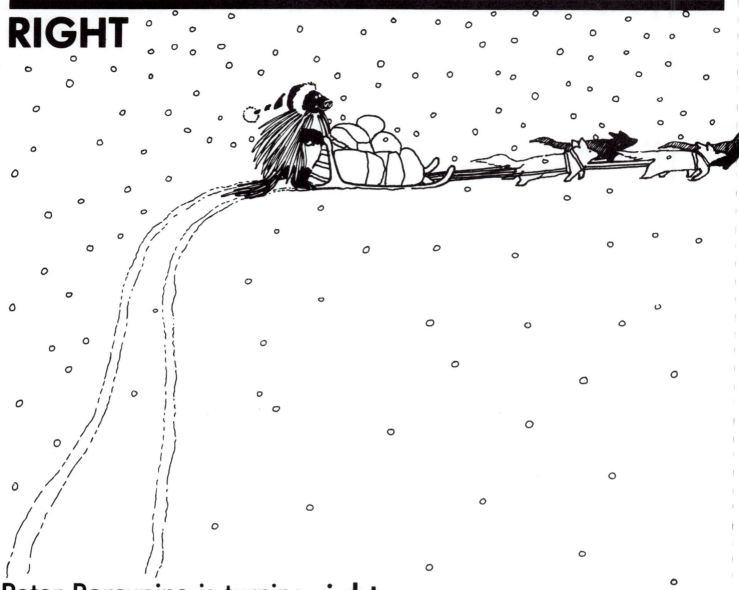

Peter Porcupine is turning right.

Circle what is turning **right**.

LEFT

Peter Porcupine must turn **left**.

Circle the sign that points **left**.

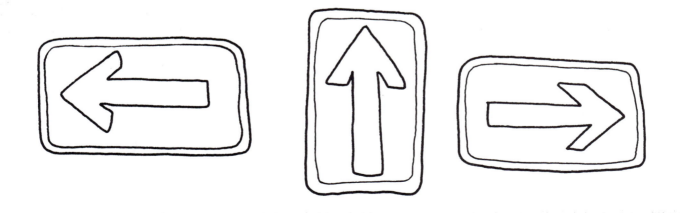

RIGHT

Peter Porcupine must turn **right**.

Circle who is pointing **right**.

214

Peter Porcupine hurt his **left** .

Circle the girl's **left** 🖐.

RIGHT

Peter Porcupine puts up his **right** .

Circle the boy's **right** .

Peter Porcupine is **next to** the .

Circle who is **next to** the .

NEXT TO

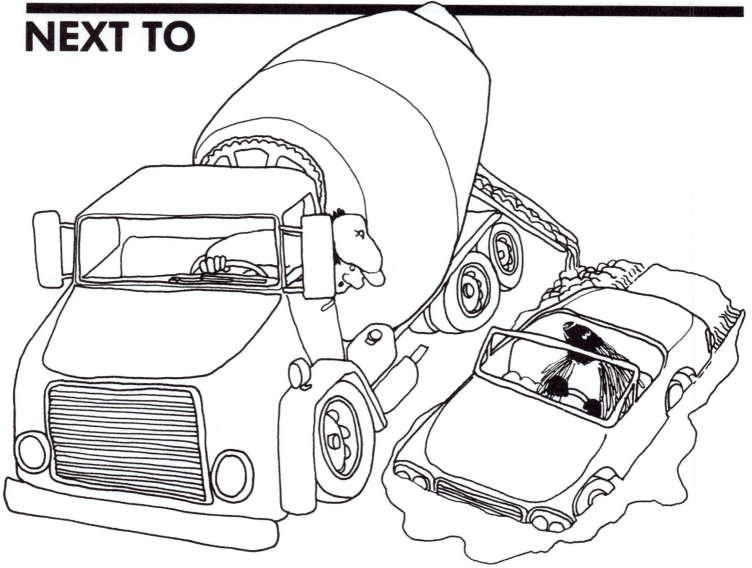

Peter Porcupine is parking **next to** the .

Circle what is **next to** the 🏪 .

218

Circle the picture that shows the same as the first picture.

up

in back of

near

Circle the picture that shows the same as the first picture.

left

down

out

Circle the picture that shows the same as the first picture.

bottom

far

on

Circle the picture that shows the same as the first picture.

in front of

over

top

Circle the picture that shows the same as the first picture.

low

right

under

Circle the picture that shows the same as the first picture.

off

high

in

CAT

Circle the picture that rhymes with the big one.

Circle the picture that rhymes with .

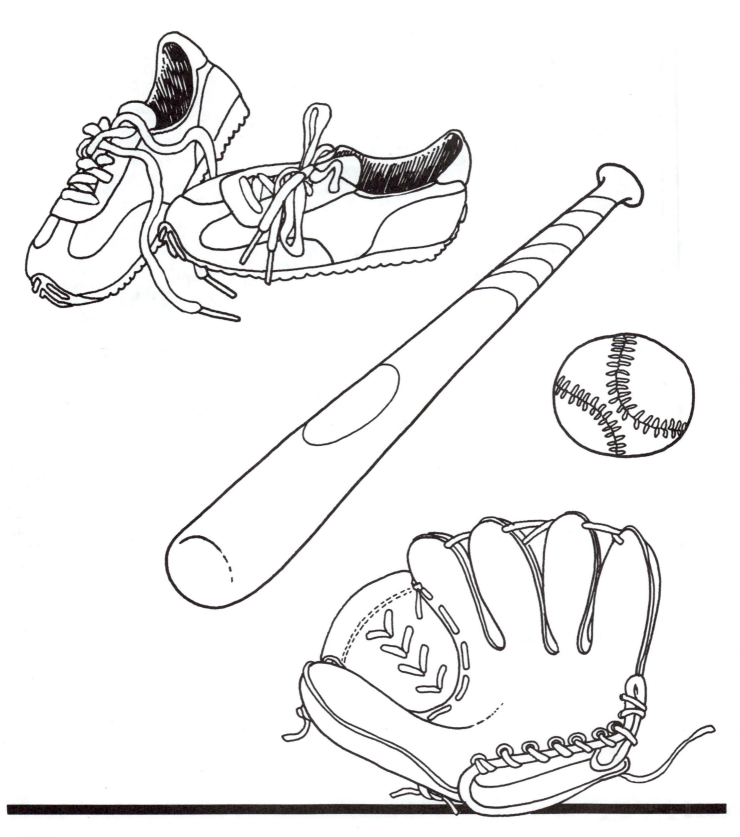

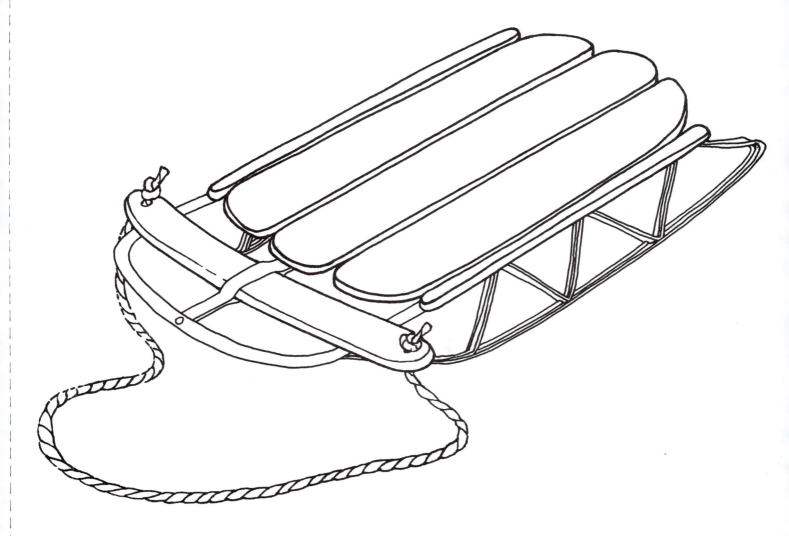

Circle the picture that rhymes with the big one. ■

Circle the picture that rhymes with  .

Circle the picture that rhymes with the big one.

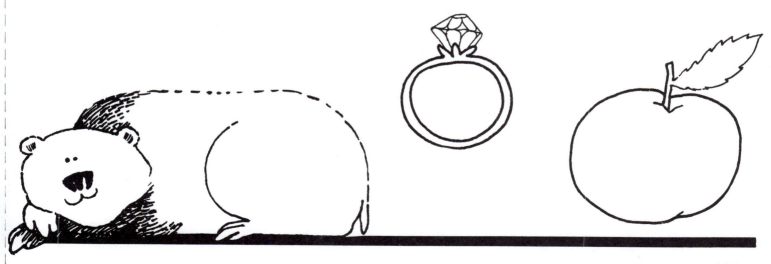

Circle the picture that rhymes with .

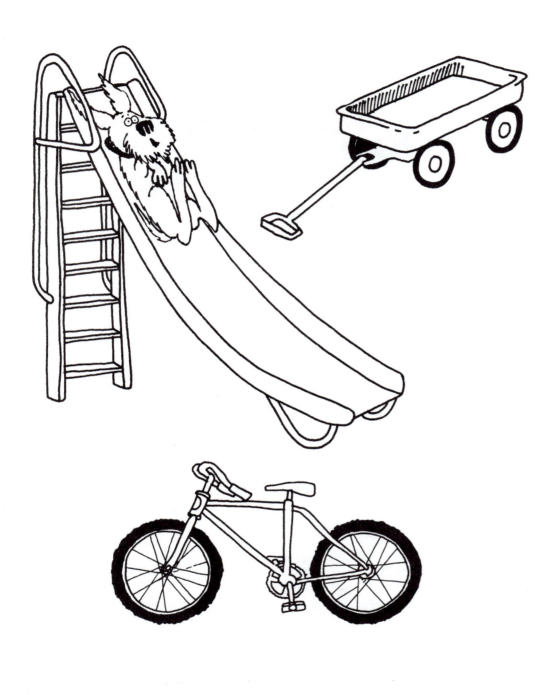

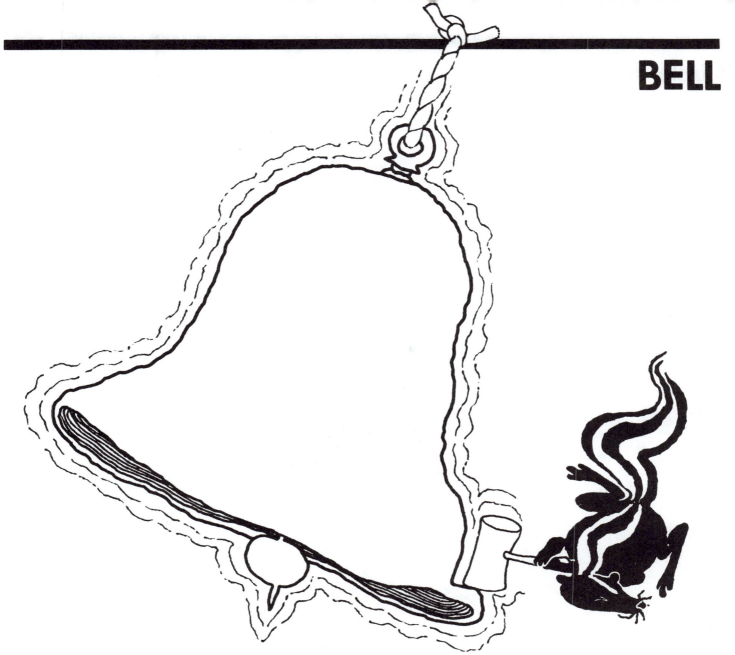

Circle the picture that rhymes with the big one.

Circle the picture that rhymes with .

GOAT

Circle the picture that rhymes with the big one.

Circle the picture that rhymes with  .

Circle the picture that rhymes with the big one.

Circle the picture that rhymes with .

BEAR

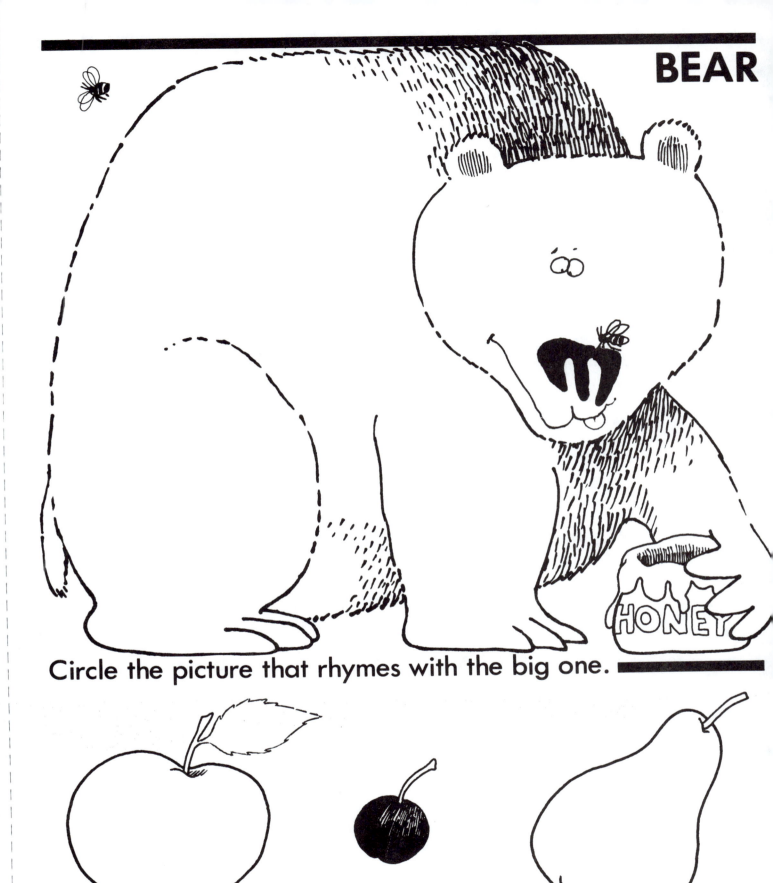

Circle the picture that rhymes with the big one.

Circle the picture that rhymes with  .

Circle the picture that rhymes with the big one. ▬▬

Circle the picture that rhymes with .

MICE

Circle the picture that rhymes with the big one.

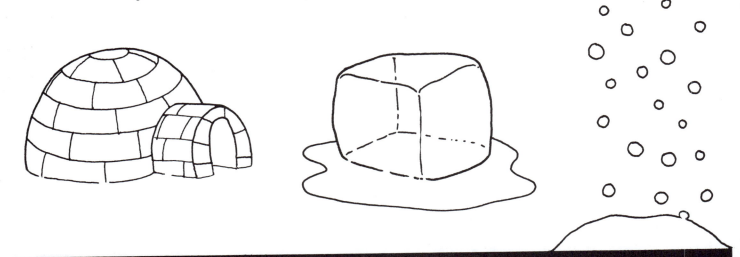

Circle the picture that rhymes with

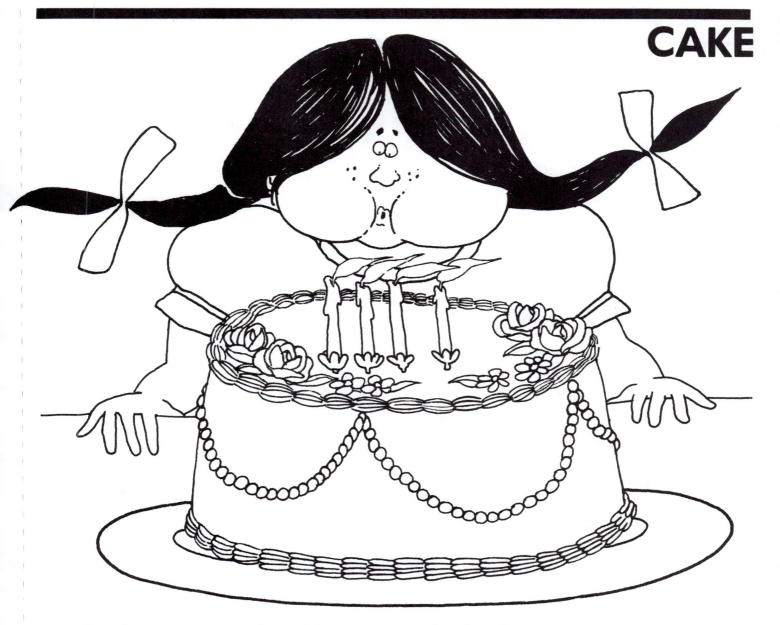

Circle the picture that rhymes with the big one.

Circle the picture that rhymes with .

DOG

Circle the picture that rhymes with the big one. ▬▬▬

245

Circle the picture that rhymes with .

FAN

Circle the picture that rhymes with the big one.

Circle the picture that rhymes with .

Circle the picture that rhymes with the big one.

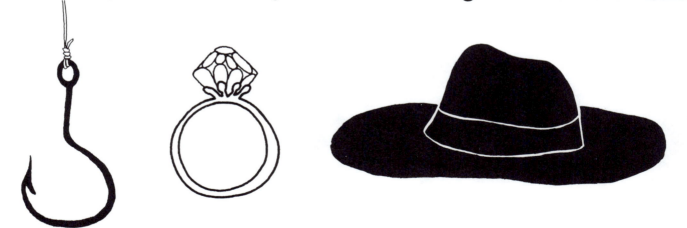

Circle the picture that rhymes with .

DRUM

Circle the picture that rhymes with the big one.

Circle the picture that rhymes with  .

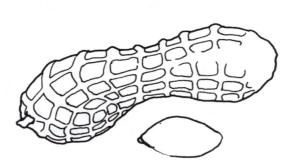

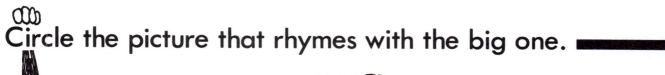
Circle the picture that rhymes with the big one.

Circle the picture that rhymes with .

TRAIN

Circle the picture that rhymes with the big one.

Circle the picture that rhymes with  .

A

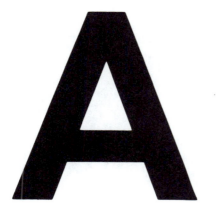

Trace **A**. Then write **A**.

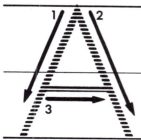

Write **A** under the picture that begins like **APPLE**.

B

BEAR

Trace **B**. Then write **B**. ▬▬▬▬▬▬▬▬▬

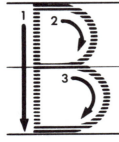

Write **B** under the picture that begins like **BEAR**. ▬▬▬

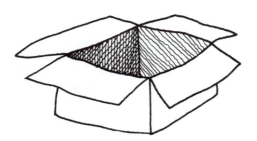

258

CAT

Trace **C**. Then write **C**.

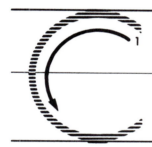

Write **C** under the picture that begins like **CAT**.

D

DUCK

Trace D. Then write D.

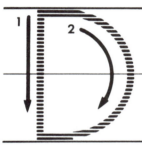

Write D under the picture that begins like DUCK.

E

ELEPHANT

Trace **E**. Then write **E**.

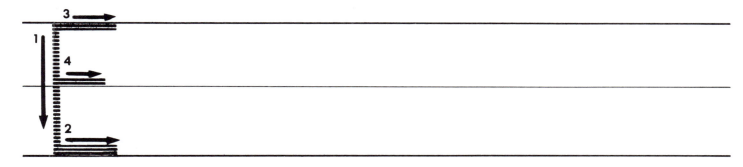

Write **E** under the picture that begins like **ELEPHANT**.

F

FISH

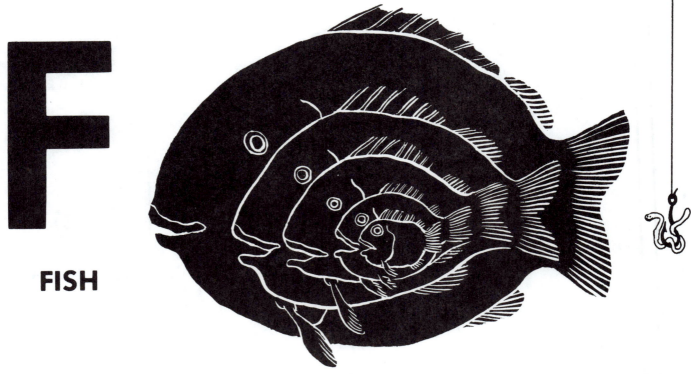

Trace **F**. Then write **F**. ▬▬▬▬▬▬▬

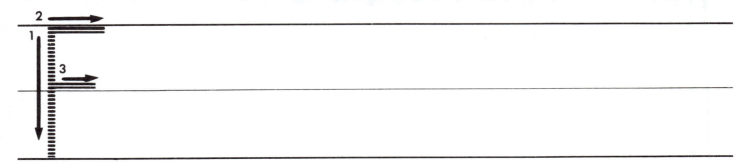

Write **F** under the picture that begins like **FISH**. ▬▬▬

262

GOAT

Trace **G**. Then write **G**.

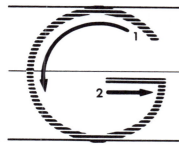

Write **G** under the picture that begins like **GOAT**.

H

HORSE

Trace **H**. Then write **H**. ▬▬▬▬▬▬▬▬▬▬▬

Write **H** under the picture that begins like **HORSE**. ▬▬▬

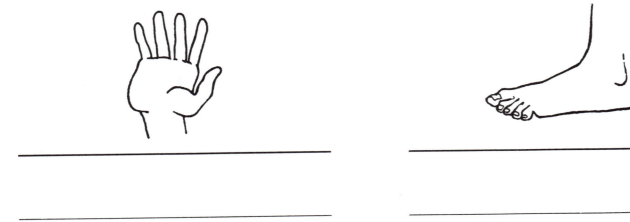

I

IGLOO

Trace I. Then write I.

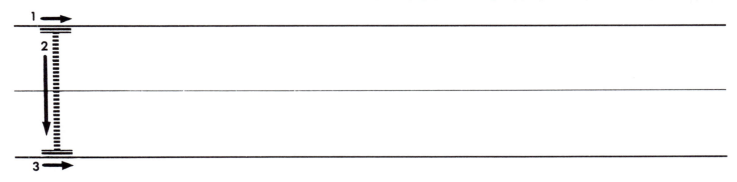

Write I under the picture that begins like IGLOO.

J

JELLY

Trace **J**. Then write **J**. ▬▬▬▬▬▬▬▬▬

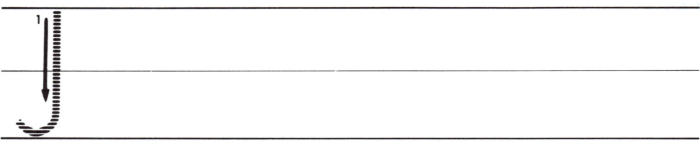

Write **J** under the picture that begins like **JELLY**. ▬▬▬▬

K

KITE

Trace K. Then write K.

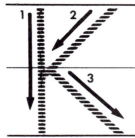

Write K under the picture that begins like KITE.

_____   _____

_____   _____

_____   _____

LION

Trace **L**. Then write **L**.

Write **L** under the picture that begins like **LION**.

MONKEY

M

Trace M. Then write M. ━━━━━━━━━━━━━━━

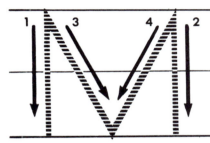

Write M under the picture that begins like MONKEY. ━━━

　　　　　　　　269

N

NEST

Trace **N**. Then write **N**.

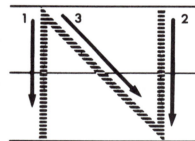

Write **N** under the picture that begins like **NEST**.

270

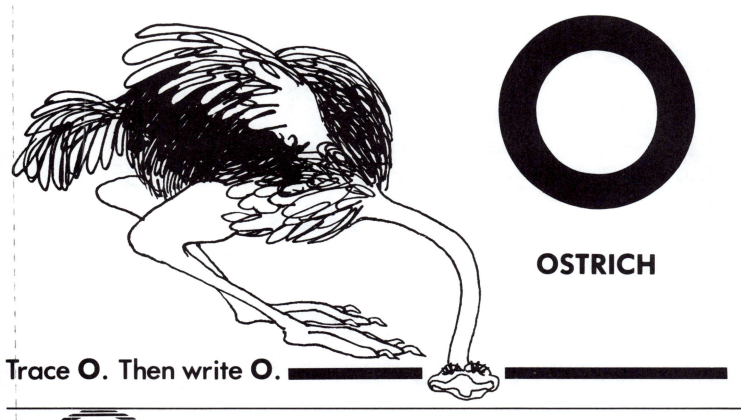

O

OSTRICH

Trace **O**. Then write **O**. ━━━━━━━ 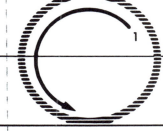 ━━━━━━━

Write **O** under the picture that begins like **OSTRICH**. ━━━━

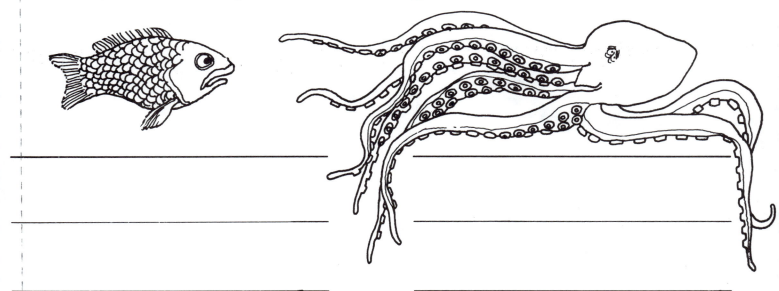

271

P

PIRATE

Trace **P**. Then write **P**.

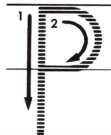

Write **P** under the picture that begins like **PIRATE**.

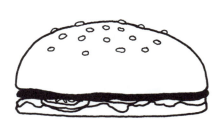

QUILT

Q

Trace Q. Then write Q. ━━━━

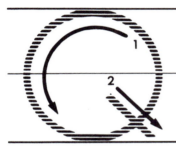

Write Q under the picture that begins like QUILT. ━━━━

R

ROOSTER

Trace R. Then write R.

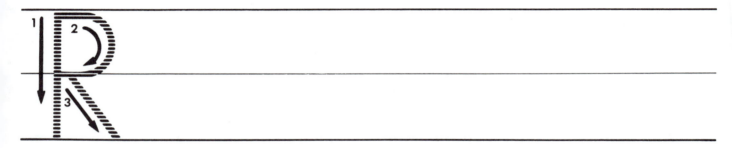

Write R under the picture that begins like ROOSTER. ▬

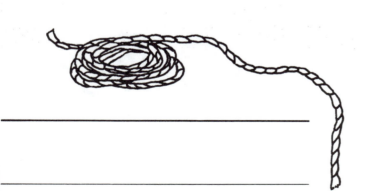

SAILBOAT

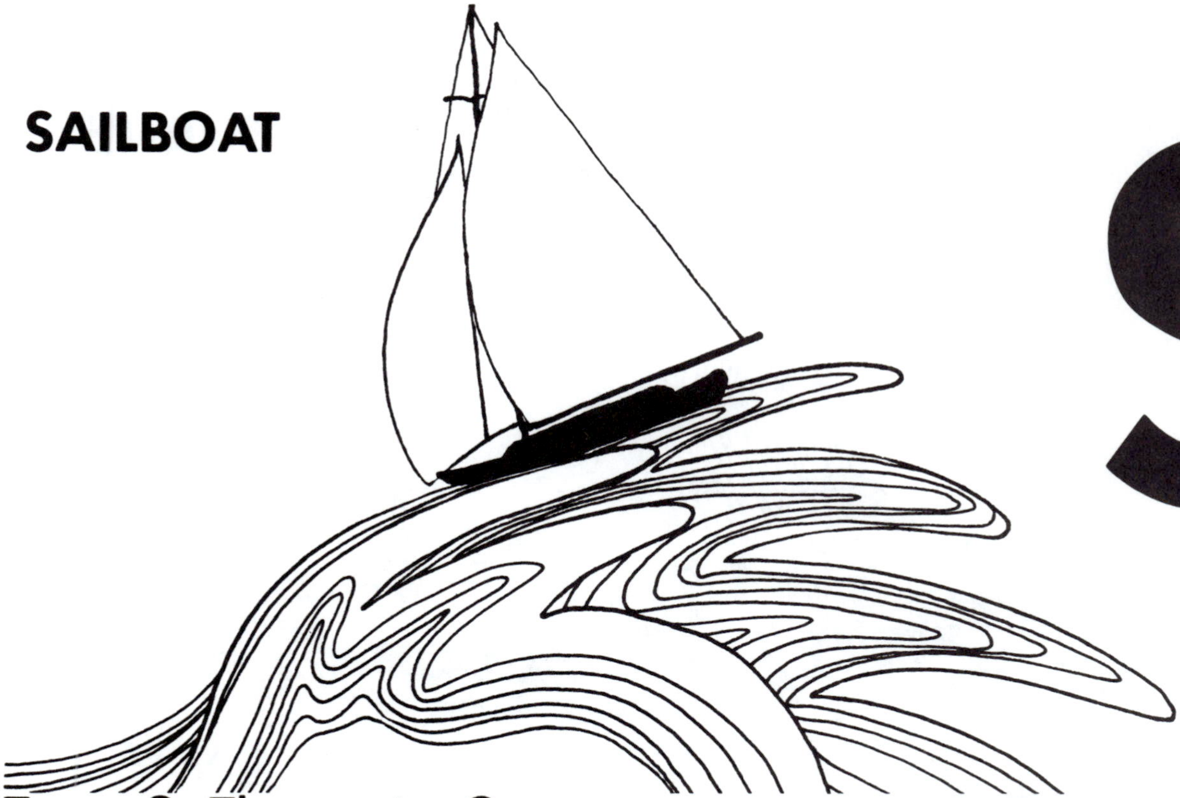

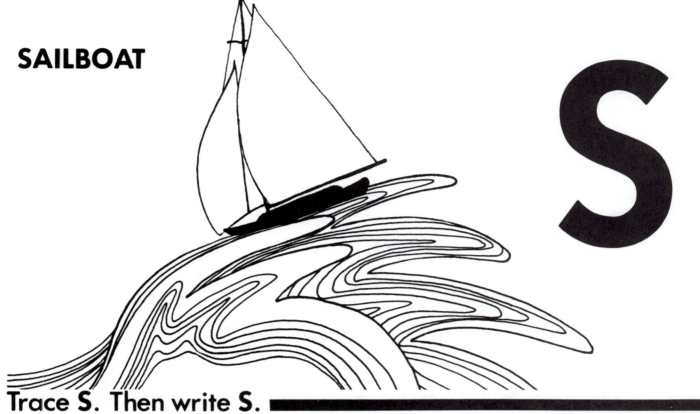

S

Trace S. Then write S.

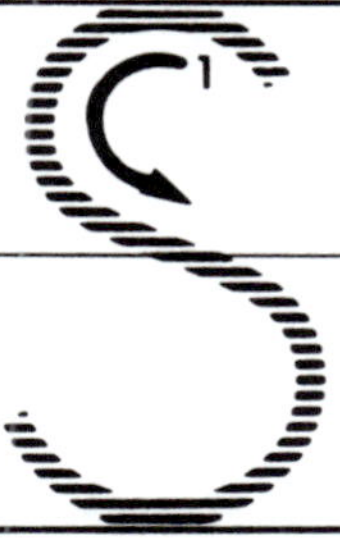

Write S under the picture that begins like SAILBOAT.

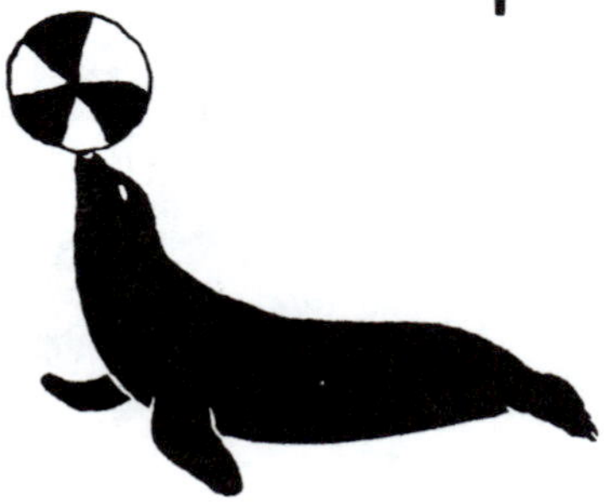

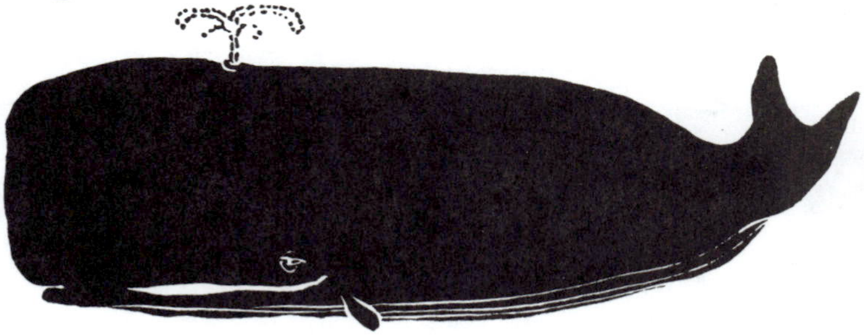

T

Trace T. Then write T.

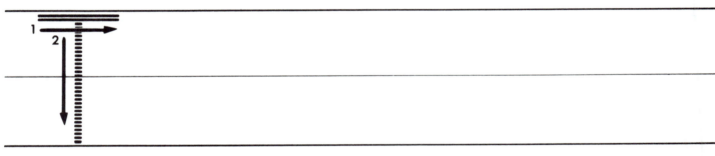

Write T under the picture that begins like TURTLE.

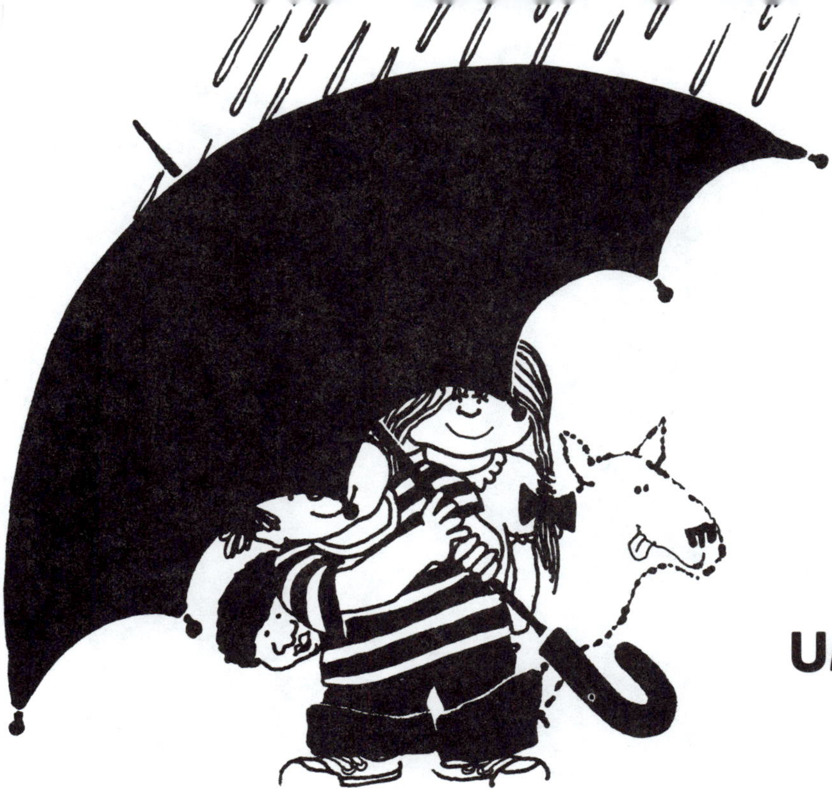

U

UMBRELLA

Trace U. Then write U.

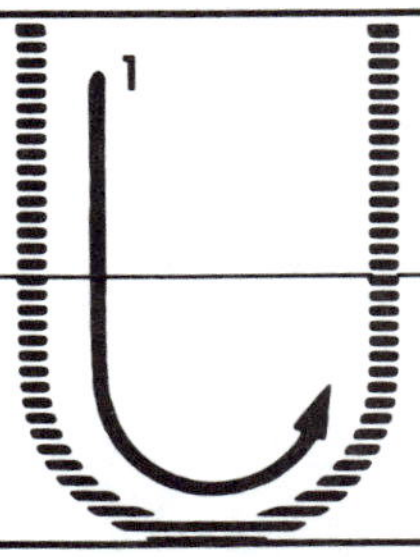

Write U under the picture that begins like UMBRELLA.

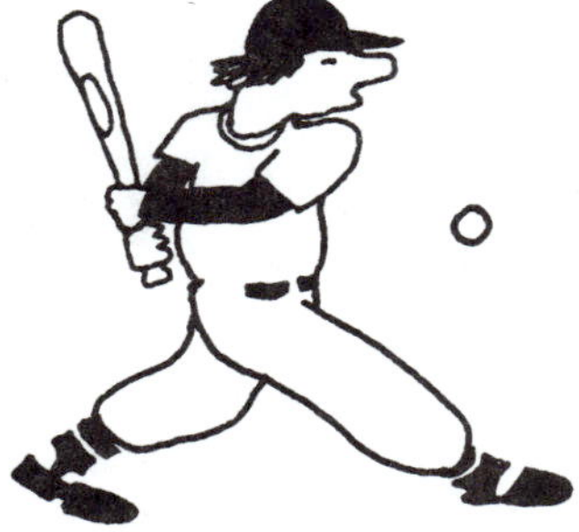

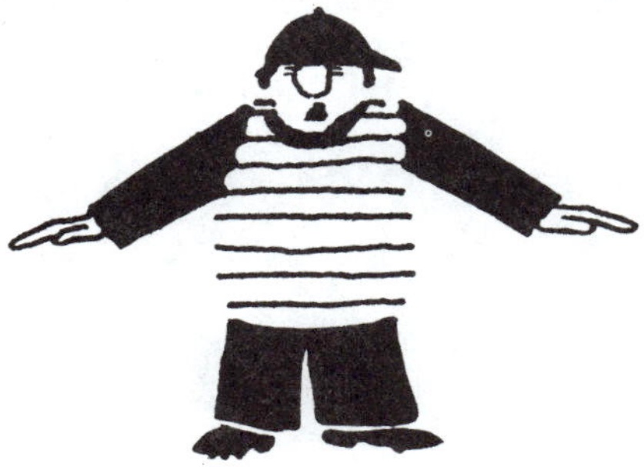

V

VEST

Trace V. Then write V. ▬▬▬▬▬▬▬▬▬▬▬▬

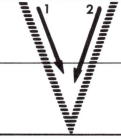

Write V under the picture that begins like VEST. ▬▬▬▬▬

W

WALRUS

Trace W. Then write W. ▬▬▬▬▬▬▬▬▬▬▬

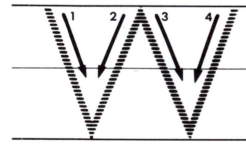

Write W under the picture that begins like WALRUS. ▬▬

279

X

X-RAY

Trace **X**. Then write **X**.

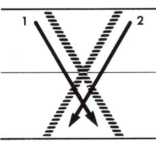

Write **X** under the picture that begins like **X-RAY**.

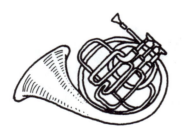

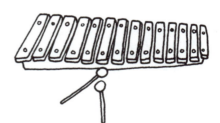

Y

YAK

Trace **Y**. Then write **Y**. ▬▬▬▬▬▬▬▬▬▬

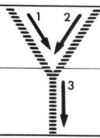

Write **Y** under the picture that begins like **YAK**. ▬▬▬

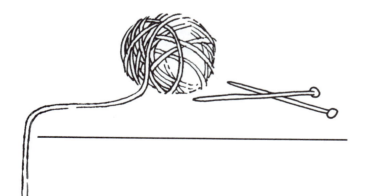

Z

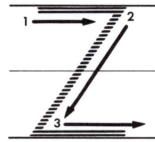

Trace Z. Then write Z.

Write Z under the picture that begins like ZEBRA.

Trace the letters. Say the name of each letter.

Circle the letter that has the beginning sound of the picture.

V
T
B
C

B
S
T
L

K
M
P
R

X
U
D
E

Draw a line from the letter to the picture that begins with that sound. Write the letter.

C

F

N

P

Draw lines to the pictures that begin with the same sound.
Trace the letters.

Circle the picture that has the beginning sound of the letter. Write the letter.

J

O

R

T

Write the letter that has the beginning sound of the picture.

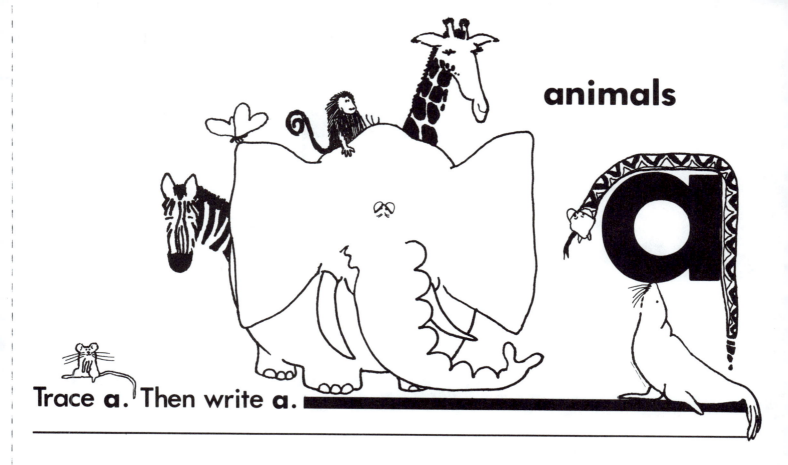

animals

Trace **a**. Then write **a**.

Write **a** to finish the picture words.

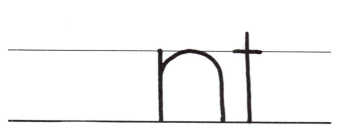

n t

h t

b

bird

Trace **b**. Then write **b**.

1 ↓ 2

Write **b** to finish the picture words.

ba y   ear

C

camel

Trace **c**. Then write **c**.

Write **c** to finish the picture words.

_at

_ar

d

doll

Trace **d**. Then write **d**.

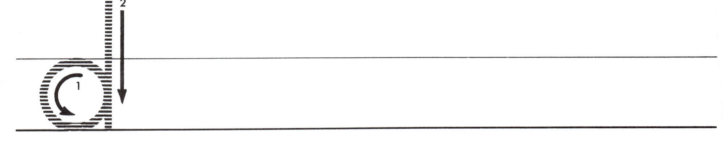

Write **d** to finish the picture words.

og

be

292

elf

Trace **e**. Then write **e**.

Write **e** to finish the picture words.

gg

b ll

f

fence

Trace **f**. Then write **f**.

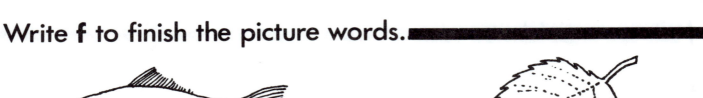

Write **f** to finish the picture words.

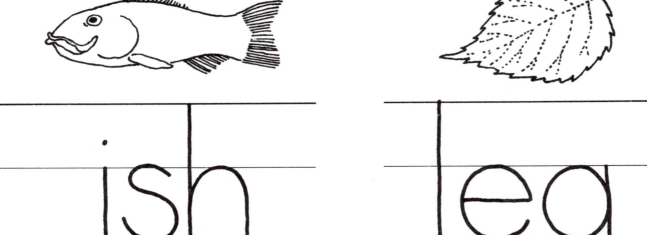

ish   ea

g

garden

Trace **g**. Then write **g**.

Write **g** to finish the picture words.

ir l

wa on

helmets

Trace **h**. Then write **h**.

Write **h** to finish the picture words.

_at   _ook

insects

Trace **i**. Then write **i**.

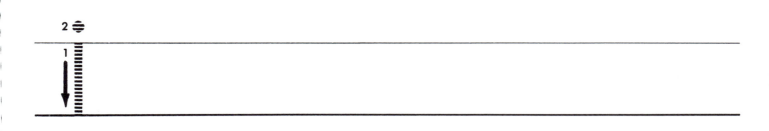

2 ⬌
1 ↓

Write **i** to finish the picture words.

f___sh

___nk

j

judge

Trace j. Then write j.

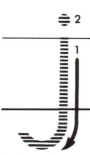

Write j to finish the picture words.

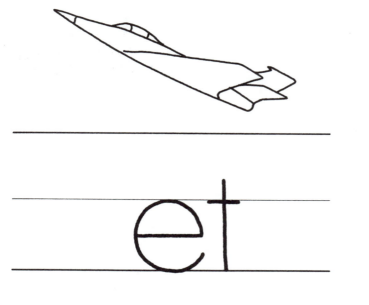

_et

_elly

k

kittens

Trace k. Then write k.

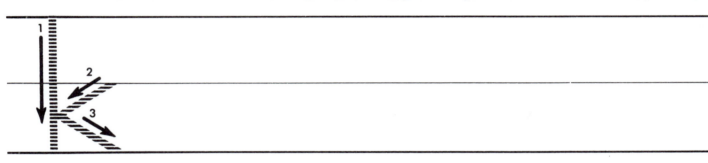

Write k to finish the picture words.

ey   boo

l

lamb

Trace **l**. Then write **l**.

Write **l** to finish the picture words.

_amp

_____ appe

300

m

marbles

Trace m. Then write m. ▬▬▬▬▬▬▬

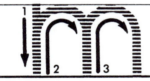

Write m to finish the picture words. ▬▬▬▬▬

ouse   dru

numbers

n

Trace n. Then write n.

Write n to finish the picture words.

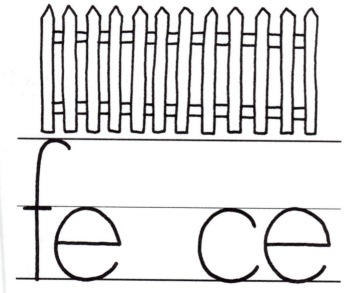

fe __ ce

__ est

302

Trace **o**. Then write **o**.

Write **o** to finish the picture words.

__ x

fr__g

p

piano

Trace **p**. Then write **p**.

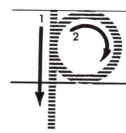

Write **p** to finish the picture words.

_ig

mo_

quail

q

Trace **q**. Then write **q**.

Write **q** to finish the picture words.

uilt

ueen

rocket

r

Trace **r**. Then write **r**. ▬▬▬▬▬▬▬▬▬▬▬▬▬▬▬▬▬

Write **r** to finish the picture words. ▬▬▬▬▬▬▬

ake   bi d

306

seven

Trace **s**. Then write **s**.

Write **s** to finish the picture words.

___eal

hor___e

t taxi

Trace **t**. Then write **t**.

Write **t** to finish the picture words.

ca_____

_____able

308

u

umbrellas

Trace **u**. Then write **u**.

Write **u** to finish the picture words.

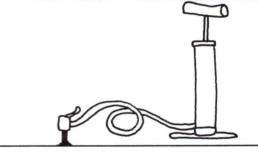

_____ p   _____ p   m p

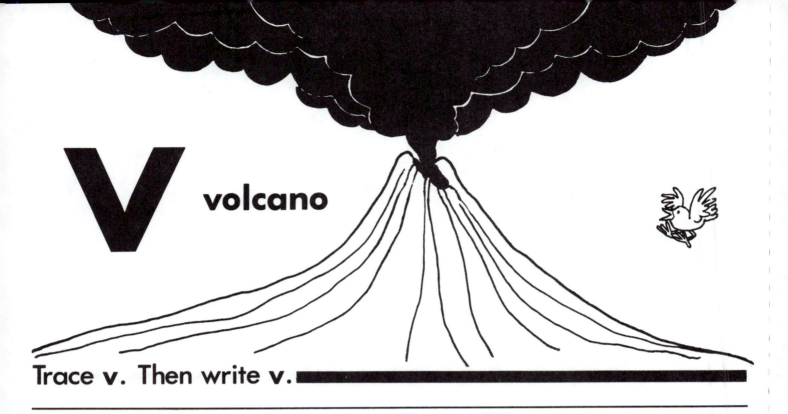

V

volcano

Trace v. Then write v. ▰▰▰▰▰▰

V

Write v to finish the picture words. ▰▰▰▰▰▰

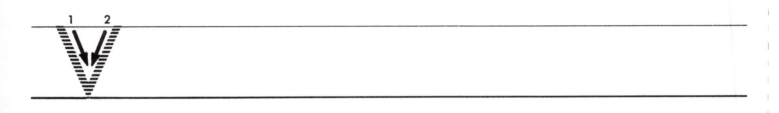

fi_e   ri_er

woman

Trace **w**. Then write **w**.

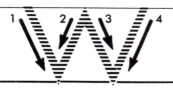

Write **w** to finish the picture words.

_____orm

_____ag

311

xylophone

X

Trace **x**. Then write **x**. ▬▬▬▬▬▬▬▬▬▬▬

Write **x** to finish the picture words. ▬▬▬▬▬▬

fo___

si___

312

yarn

Trace **y**. Then write **y**.

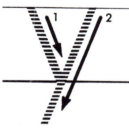

Write **y** to finish the picture words.

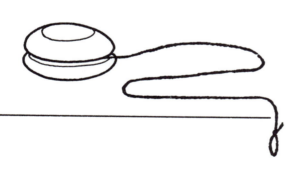

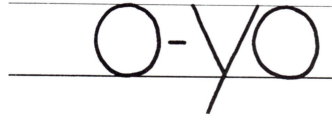

o-yo

awn

zipper

Trace **z**. Then write **z**.

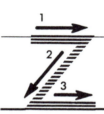

Write **z** to finish the picture words.

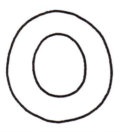

_ero

_ebra

Trace the letters. Say the name of each letter.

Write the correct letter to finish each picture word.

e d r

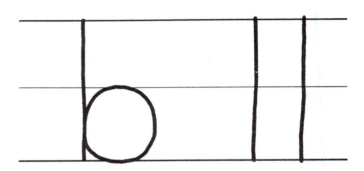

b _ ll

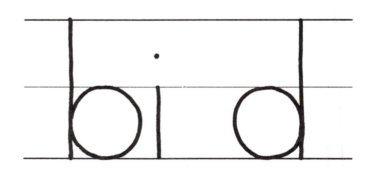

b i _ d

_ o g

316

Write the correct letter to finish each picture word.

p a h

c _ t

mo _

_ ook

Write the correct letter to finish each picture word.

c m o

fr___g

dru___

___ar